AWESOME MINDS

VIDEO GAME CREATORS

Library of Congress Cataloging-in-Publication Data available upon request.
HC ISBN: 978-1-947458-22-2, PB ISBN: 978-1-947458-48-2

duopress books are available at special discounts when purchased in bulk for sales promotions as well as for fund-raising or educational use. Special editions can be created to specification.

Contact us at hello@duopressbooks.com for more information.

This book is an independent, unauthorized, and unofficial biography and account of the people involved in the development and history of video games and is not affiliated with, endorsed by, or sponsored by Activision Publishing Inc.; Amazon.com, Inc.; Ampex Data Systems Corporation; Apple Inc.; Atari, SA; Backbone Entertainment; BAE Systems Inc.; BlackBerry Limited; Blizzard Entertainment, Inc.; British Broadcasting Corporation; Capcom Co., Ltd.; Chuck E. Cheese's; Coleco Holdings, LLC; Commodore International; Dave & Buster's, Inc.; Dimps Corporation; Duolingo; EA Maxis; Electronic Arts Inc.; Entertainment Software Rating Board; General Motors Company; Gillette; Google LLC; Graphics Properties Holdings, Inc.; Hearst Communications Inc.; Houghton Mifflin Harcourt; Kickstarter, PBC; KinderCare Education; Konami Holdings Corporation; LeapFrog Enterprises, Inc.; LucasArts Entertainment Company, LLC; Magnavox; Matchbox; Mattel, Inc.; Microsoft Corporation; Mojang AB; Motorola, Inc.; Namco Limited; Niantic, Inc.; Nintendo, Co. Ltd.; Nintendo of America; Nokia Oyj; Oculus VR, LLC; Other Ocean Group Inc.; RadioShack; Rare; Rovio Entertainment Corporation; Sears, Roebuck, and Company; Sega Sammy Holdings Inc.; Sega Games Co., Ltd.; Sega of America; Silicon Graphics International Corp.; Skee-Ball; SIMS Co., Ltd.; Sony Corporation; Square Enix Holdings Co., Ltd.; Sumo Digital Ltd.; Taito Corporation; Tetris Holding; Time Warner, Inc.; Valve Corporation; Vivendi SA.; WMS Industries, Inc.; World Almanac; Xerox Corporation; Yamaha Corporation; YouTube, LLC; or any other person or entity owning or controlling rights in their name, trademark, or copyrights.

Any product names, logos, trademarks, trade names, brands, characters, or images depicted and referred to herein are the property of their respective owners and are used solely to identify the particular video game or invention with which such product names, logos, trademarks, trade names, brands, character, or images are associated.

Cover inspired by *Space Invaders*.

Manufactured in China
10 9 8 7 6 5 4 3 2 1
Duopress LLC
8 Market Place, Suite 300, Baltimore, MD 21202
Distributed by Workman Publishing Company, Inc.

Published simultaneously in Canada by Thomas Allen & Son Limited.
To order: hello@duopressbooks.com
www.duopressbooks.com
www.workman.com

AWESOME MINDS

VIDEO GAME CREATORS

BY

ALEJANDRO ARBONA

ART BY

CHELSEA O'MARA HOLEMAN

duopress

We asked the author:
Who is your video game hero?

In my personal opinion, Shigeru Miyamoto is the greatest creative mind ever to work in video games, the most imaginative designer ever to create a game, the canniest storyteller, and the most reliable hit-maker video games ever had. In this book you'll read about just a few of the legendary games he created, single-handedly. He is a personal hero of mine.

—Alejandro Arbona

Now, we ask you:
Who is your video game hero?

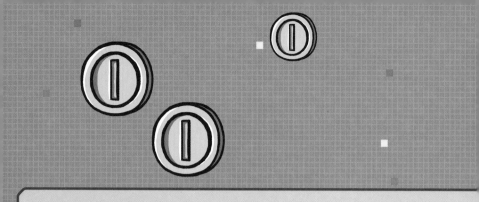

CONTENTS

INTRODUCTION
LET'S GET THIS STARTED

The video games we play today come in many unique
forms: as consoles for our TV, streaming online through
our home computers, downloaded to portable devices
like our phones and tablets, and even the fully immersive environment inside a virtual reality headset. But
however we enter those worlds, video games all have
one thing in common—the computer. People used computers to create all these games, and the devices we
play them on are all computers of one kind or another.

The creation of video games stretches back almost as
far as the invention of the modern computer. If you dig
deep enough into their history, some of the very first
video games were played in the late 1940s and early
1950s. Engineers and programmers, mostly working
in labs at universities and military contractors (private
companies working for the United
States government), designed rudimentary digital games to demonstrate
how their new inventions were interactive—you would press a key and a
blip moved on the screen.

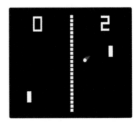

Pong is one of the earliest
arcade video games.

The evolution of computers actually began long before that. It happened very slowly over a hundred years, starting in the year 1837. A man named Charles Babbage designed what he called the "Analytical Engine," a machine that could do calculations automatically. In 1843, a woman named Ada Lovelace wrote an algorithm, a series of actions for the Analytical Engine to execute, making her the world's first computer programmer. Babbage never finished a practical build of the Analytical Engine, and so Lovelace's algorithm was never tested; nevertheless, what they created together were the ideas that became the modern computer more than a century later.

Mathematician
Ada Lovelace

The advances that were made in modern computing—and video games—came at blinding speed. From the middle of the 20th century until today, computers and video games developed so fast that no one could ever predict how the new technology would look in 10 years. Computers in the 1950s were so big, they filled entire rooms, and computer technicians would interact with walls of noisy processors grinding through their calculations. By the 1960s, technicians at labs like Xerox in Palo Alto, California, had made devices compact enough to be called "personal computers," though they were still the size of a washing machine and you had to be a trained expert to operate one. Ten years after that, by the '70s, computers became small enough that a person could put one on their desk at work and write a letter.

 By the middle of the 1980s, more and more people had computers in their homes, with early black-and-white video games and interchangeable floppy disks (the icon we still use today to represent "save") to store information. Not only that, there were dedicated video game consoles like the ones made by Atari and Nintendo; computers had become so common that special machines were manufactured and sold just for play. Modems and the World Wide Web began to enter our lives. By the '90s, the home computer was a staple for every middle-class family, now equipped with email, web browsers, and games on CD-ROM featuring slick, colorful, highly rendered graphics. Video game consoles, too, brought us the high-powered, candy-colored games of Super Nintendo and Sega Genesis. And during the first decades of the 21st century, we've witnessed a technology boom in our own living rooms—graphics and sound as detailed and evocative as a movie, massive multiplayer virtual worlds, online streaming, and real-time interaction with other gamers.

The small computers we carry around nowadays—our phones and tablets—have more processing power in their tiny chips than those rooms full of computers at university labs did in the 1950s. Today we use computers to talk to friends all over the world, work, learn, shop, watch TV and movies...and of course, play video games. Let's take a look at how we got here.

EVERYTHING STARTED...
AS A GAME

From table tennis to a war in space, and back again—as the first computers are powered up, video games are born, and the world will never be the same.

Asteroids, an Atari arcade game designed by Ed Logg, Lyle Rains, and Dominic Walsh, released in 1979

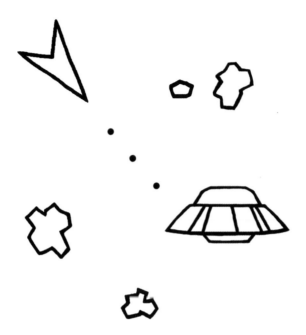

Before creating the world's first video game, William Higinbotham helped the American government build the atomic bomb that was used in World War II. As a physicist, Higinbotham had been recruited to lead the electronics department for the Manhattan Project, the top-secret scientific operation to split the atom and turn it into a weapon. He spent the rest of his career after the war at the Brookhaven National Laboratory in Long Island, New York, creating sophisticated instrumentation for the U.S. Department of Energy.

Brookhaven Lab held a public exhibition every year to demonstrate its latest developments. As the research facility prepared for its 1958 show, Higinbotham saw that Brookhaven's brand-new model of computer could use its processing power to calculate wind resistance and simulate the trajectory of an object moving through the air. This could be useful for all kinds of practical purposes, like aircraft design and missile defense, but Higinbotham had a more fun idea for how to show off what the computer could do.

In a matter of hours, he designed a game called *Tennis for Two*, then sat down to build it with the help of a technician on staff, Robert Dvorak. They made custom handheld controllers out of aluminum, with a knob on the top. For the game's display, they hooked their computer up to an oscilloscope, a device with a round screen that shows a digital wave representing electric voltage. Turning the knob, two players could "hit" a ten-nis ball—represented by a glowing blip—back and forth; each "swing" tweaked the voltage inside the oscilloscope so the "ball" seemed to sail across the screen.

WAR GAMES

There was a huge effort to drive technology forward during World War II, and as a result, the United States was suddenly full of young engineers and inventors working for the government after the war ended in 1945. Their efforts went into overdrive when, in 1957, Russia took the U.S. by surprise and launched the world's first satellite, Sputnik. This kicked off the Space Race, and the U.S. rushed to develop computers, build rockets, and invent new and faster ways to communicate.

The government started the Advanced Research Projects Agency (ARPA) in 1958 to focus on these efforts; ARPA ended up creating the American space program (later spun off into NASA) and inventing the internet. Engineers at ARPA and at private government contractors would practice national defense by using computer simulators to shoot down imaginary missiles; these were early video games, meant only for top-secret government use and not for the public.

With a whole generation of new engineers, and an incentive to invent—winning the Space Race and keeping a leading edge in the Cold War against the Soviet Union—computers evolved very, very quickly.

Tennis for Two was a smash hit at the Brookhaven exhibition, drawing crowds of players and spectators. It was the first video game; other interactive computer programs already existed—technology companies working for the government had created missile-defense simulators, and academic research labs had simple digital interfaces like tic-tac-toe and an electronic stylus to move a dot on-

THE PDP-1

Mainframe computers aren't the kind of machine you'd have at home. Today, they're the computers used by big companies for all their large, automated calculation jobs—any kind of massive number crunching for data, statistics, and transactions. For example, when you order books from Amazon.com, rows of mainframe computers scan your order details, update the records of the warehouse inventory, and calculate the company's profits.

But in the early 1960s, when MIT acquired the Programmed Data Processor-1, "mainframe" referred to any of the new kind of computer that housed its memory and its central processing unit (the computer's "brain") in its own stand-alone cabinet instead of running on several machines that filled a whole room.

The PDP-1 was built in 1959 by Digital Equipment Corporation and intended for use by government research labs. It was the first computer specifically designed to facilitate interactivity with its operator, lending itself easily for tinkering and innovation by clever and inventive users. It ended up becoming the first mainframe computer used for word processing, composing digital music...and video games.

screen through a maze, just to demonstrate how their machines were interactive—but *Tennis for Two* was meant for the public to play, and it was designed to entertain them. It wasn't for sale in stores or available to play at arcades, but it would inspire countless other game designers after it...including a much more famous table tennis game. But more on that later.

Three years after the splash of *Tennis for Two*, the members of the Tech Model Railroad Club at the Massachusetts Institute of Technology (MIT)—a group involved with computers, technology, and the birth of hacker culture—were exploring the capabilities of the Programmed Data Processor-1, a sophisticated mainframe computer that had been donated to the school for young engineers to tinker with.

The massive machine cost over a hundred thousand dollars—roughly a hundred times more than your typical Apple laptop today. The PDP-1 could simulate forces such as gravity, and these young people, led by Steve Russell, dreamed up a way to incorporate this into a video game. They designed *Spacewar!*, a game pitting two spaceships—a needle and a wedge made of simple white lines on a black background—in a torpedo battle

TENNIS FOR TWO

Along with the world's first video game, William Higinbotham gave us the world's first video game controller in 1958—a handheld aluminum box with a circular knob on the top.

SPACEWAR!

Alan Kotok and Bob Saunders helped refine *Spacewar!* at MIT, and they improved on the game in 1962 by creating rudimentary gamepads with toggle switches—a forerunner of the arcade joystick.

LASER CLAY SHOOTING SYSTEM

The revolutionary toy light-beam zapper invented by Gunpei Yokoi for Nintendo led the company to create the world's first video game shooter in 1973.

GRAN TRAK 10

Atari put the player in the driver's seat, equipping this 1974 video game cabinet with a steering wheel—the standard for arcade driving games to this day.

ATARI 2600

Incorporating the intuitive joystick-and-button interface that had become popular at arcades, Atari's pioneering controller for the 2600 console brought the joystick home in 1977.

MISSILE COMMAND

The trackball controller invented for *Missile Command* in 1980 didn't become a big part of arcade video games, but it was a forerunner of the mouse that would soon become a key accessory of home computers.

GAME & WATCH

Gunpei Yokoi flattened the joystick into a four-arrow directional pad for these portable Nintendo devices, starting with *Donkey Kong* in 1982, establishing the model it would use with the NES and other consoles for decades to come.

SONY PLAYSTATION

Exploring video game worlds took on a new dimension when the Sony PlayStation installed a second joystick in 1995, and Microsoft Xbox followed soon after, controlling a character's viewpoint independent of their movement.

NINTENDO 64

After more than 10 years and several consoles, Nintendo broke with its own tradition of the "D-pad" in 1996, adding a third handle with an optional joystick, plus a slot for a Rumble Pak—an add-on to make the controller rumble in a player's hands.

NINTENDO Wii

In 2006, after a decade of increasingly complex controllers, Nintendo changed the game again by adding a laser sensor for intuitive gameplay; players could use the cordless "Wiimote" like a classic Nintendo Entertainment System (NES) two-handed gamepad, swing it like a tennis racket, or point it at the screen like a gun.

as they're dragged around in space by the gravity of a white star in the middle of the screen. The ships could be steered by the players, but they also moved on their own, drifting in a decaying orbit as the star's gravity pulled them closer.

Like *Tennis for Two, Spacewar!* wasn't available commercially, but it became extremely popular among the small communities of programmers, computer hobbyists, and students at MIT and other universities around the country. As it spread, other developers fine-tuned their own versions of the game or added features. For example, players initially steered their ships and fired torpedoes by toggling rigid switches right on the front of the computer itself; but Alan Kotok and Bob Saunders, two members of MIT's Tech Model Railroad Club who helped develop *Spacewar!*, thought it would be easier to play with handheld controllers, and they built a prototype gamepad, connected to the computer with wires. Along with William Higinbotham's knob controller for *Tennis for Two*, these were precursors of the joysticks and gamepads we still use to play video games today.

The early years of video game development were shaped at universities and research labs, by techies and programmers seeing each other's inventions and finding inspiration to take these ideas further. The vacuum of outer space in particular, with its eternal darkness, lent itself easily to the empty black screens that computers had at the time and sparked the imaginations of programmers who dreamed of their own minimal white spaceships and stars. That's why it didn't take long at all for copies and derivations to fill the newly born video game market. *Tennis for Two* and *Spacewar!* would soon inspire the games that broke out of the academic world and moved into arcades, where the public would eagerly pop in quarters to play.

THE DIGITAL SPACE RACE

Nolan Bushnell had been a student in the 1960s at the University of Utah, where he discovered *Spacewar!* at his campus computer lab. He loved the game, and he dreamed of a way to turn it into a commercial machine that players could use— for pay—at public venues. During

Nolan Bushnell

summers while he was in college, Bushnell worked at amusement parks, and he was familiar with the appeal of coin-operated games like pinball. But the technology to mass-produce a commercial video game wasn't quite there yet; the cheapest computer available still cost $4,000, and it couldn't update the graphics on the screen fast enough for the game to keep moving smoothly. Saving his idea for later, Bushnell went to work as an engineer at a government contractor, Ampex Corporation, after graduating. He kept talking with technology developers about his idea, and in 1971, when he learned that a company called Nutting Associates was producing coin-operated electronic quiz machines, he left Ampex to join them and finish developing his game.

Around the same time, two students at Stanford University in California, Bill Pitts and Hugh Tuck, were developing their own version of a coin-operated space game for commercial release. Like Bushnell, Pitts and Tuck had played *Spacewar!* at school and saw a way to create a game like it for the whole world to play. When Bushnell heard the two students were working on a game similar to his, they all met to see if they could join forces—or at least to get an idea of what the other guys were doing. Their ideas were remarkably similar, but the three men just weren't on the same page about how to execute their vision. They went their separate ways so each could chase their own ideas. It was a digital space race.

Working separately, Bushnell and the team of Pitts and Tuck had each created a remarkably similar concept: a freestanding cabinet as tall as a person, with a computer inside and a TV mounted in the front, to install in a public venue where customers could feed it coins and buy plays—the first two commercial video games. Pitts and Tuck designed and built a game called, unoriginally, *Galaxy Game*. (This early in the history of video games, names hadn't yet gotten that clever.) To their credit, they finished their game and debuted their machine first. They installed their game at the student union on campus at Stanford in September of 1971, charging ten cents for one game and a quarter for three. It was a huge hit with students, who would line up for an hour to play. However, the student union on campus wasn't exactly a public venue, and not that many people outside the university had a chance to check out *Galaxy Game.*

Nolan Bushnell, working at Nutting, took advantage of the company's existing connections to sell coin-operated entertainments and launched his own version of *Spacewar!*—with the uninspired name of *Computer Space*—at the Dutch Goose bar, near the campus of Stanford in November 1971. In his game, Bushnell had simplified the gameplay of *Spacewar!* (making it all the easier for tipsy bar patrons to get into the game after a couple of beers) and added a field of stars throughout the screen for more dazzle. Pitts and Tuck had beaten Bushnell to the market by two months with *Galaxy Game*, but because Bushnell installed *Computer Space* in a public place, he got more people to play his game...and got a lot more change out of their pockets. Even though Bushnell lost the race, he won in the end.

Nolan Bushnell, Bill Pitts, and Hugh Tuck all imagined a freestanding, coin-operated video game cabinet, but while they were racing to develop it, another visionary was working on something much smaller—and in the long run, much bigger.

THE FIRST HOME
VIDEO GAME CONSOLE

Ralf Henry Baer was born Rudolf Heinrich Baer in
Germany. As a teenager, he fled with his family to
America during the violent rise of the Nazi regime, only
a year before the start of World War II. Baer ended
up in New York, where he studied radio and television
technology and eventually got a job at a government
technology contractor called Loral Electronics. It was
1951, and technology developers could see a huge
new business coming over the horizon: television. Baer
and his coworkers were tasked with creating a TV set
from scratch for the company to manufacture and sell.
During their project, Baer would test how the screen
was working with equipment that drew vertical and
horizontal lines on it. He wondered if he could install
that function within the TV itself, for its owners to

play with when they weren't watching
something. In effect, he dreamed
of a TV game for the home.
Nobody at Loral cared for that
idea, and Baer shelved it in
the back of his mind for over a
decade.

Fifteen years later, in 1966, Baer was working for a military contractor called Sanders Associates. He had never stopped thinking about his half-baked idea for a TV game, and now he started to imagine how he could actually use Sanders's technology to create one. But Sanders only developed technology for the military, so Baer started developing his project secretly. He drafted two of the company's technicians, Bill Harrison and Bill Rusch, and assigned them to work on his pet project, code-named Channel LP ("LP" for "Let's Play").

When he had a prototype, Baer revealed his secret project to Sanders Associates. The company actually liked the idea and encouraged him to develop it further—but since it had no crossover in the market of television sets, it couldn't find a way to sell it. A few years later, in 1969, Baer personally pitched his updated prototype—which he called "the Brown Box"—to several TV set manufacturers. Magnavox hired Ralf Baer and his two technicians, and in 1972, they launched the Magnavox Odyssey—the world's first home video game console.

The Odyssey came bundled with 12 games preprogrammed in it, including, most notably, *Ping-Pong*, a successor to

Higinbotham's *Tennis for Two*. The basic idea was the same: using handheld controllers with a knob on the top, two players moved narrow, rectangular "paddles" up and down each side of a black screen to bat a square white blip back and forth across a center line. Sound familiar? Like *Spacewar!* before it, *Ping-Pong* would go on to inspire Nolan Bushnell to create another remarkably similar (and vastly more successful) game: *Pong*.

Building on the success of his *Computer Space* game, Nolan Bushnell and a partner, Ted Dabney, started a new company called Syzygy. When it turned out that name was taken, Bushnell came up with a new name: Atari. Hiring promising young developers and programmers, Bushnell's company became one of the leaders in a booming new market. (Two young programmers whom Bushnell hired, Steve Jobs and Steve Wozniak, got along so well while they developed an Atari game called *Breakout* that they went into business for themselves; they built their own computer in Wozniak's garage and named their new company Apple Computer.)

Steve Jobs & Steve Wozniak

On the very day that Bushnell founded Atari Incorporated, he hired his first technician, a young engineer named Al Alcorn, whom Bushnell had met as a trainee back at Ampex. For his first project, Bushnell assigned Alcorn a training exercise: develop a commercial, coin-operated version of *Ping-Pong,* the game he'd seen at a Magnavox demonstration. But Bushnell and Alcorn didn't just copy the existing *Ping-Pong* game; they made it better. For starters they made the name catchier—*Pong* just sounds cooler than *Ping-Pong.* Alcorn also added sound effects and a score counter, and he programmed the game so the ball would bounce at a greater variety of angles, depending on how it hit the paddles. This made *Pong* much more challenging... and much more entertaining; when one of their test machines broke down (installed, again, at a bar), Alcorn went to repair it, only to find that the reason it stopped working was because it was jammed full of quarters, from people playing it so much. By then, Bushnell had made a deal for Atari to develop a driving game for the pinball machine maker Bally Midway; but when he showed Bally Midway *Pong* instead, and it passed, he decided Atari should take a chance on the early success of its test versions and mass-produce *Pong* itself. The gamble paid off, and *Pong* went on to sell 8,000 units.

THE GAME GOES GLOBAL

The floodgates opened. Now that the first games were becoming so successful, video game companies opened shop everywhere. In Japan, a new company called Taito produced its own version of *Pong* called *Elepong*. It was Japan's first arcade video game, but since technology was already a booming industry there, dozens of electronics professionals were ready to go into business and embrace video games with a passion. New companies like Sega, Namco, and Konami, which would go on to become titans of video games, sprang up in Japan. Nintendo, a Japanese card game company that had existed since 1889 (and that had tried selling countless different products and services along the way), opened a video game division.

In the span of just a few months between 1971 and 1972, the small world of video games became massive. What had started with just *Computer Space* became an entire galaxy. Video games were big business, virtually overnight, and now the golden age of arcades was dawning.

YOU NEED COINS. A LOT OF
COINS

What began as one video game in the corner of a bar grows to dozens packed in rows at the arcade—and kids all over the world discover a new place to hang out.

Centipede arcade game, Atari, 1981

When we say "arcade games" today, we usually mean video games: the coin-operated cabinets that now exist all over the world. But other versions of "arcade games" existed before the phrase "video games" took over.

In the early 1900s, a lot of cities had midways, amuse-ment parks, and pleasure promenades, like New York's Coney Island, Copenhagen's Tivoli Gardens, and Tokyo's Hanayashiki. Places like these started to host attractions such as merry-go-rounds and the first of what were called arcade games: shooting galleries with pellet guns, ball-tossing games, and coin-operated machines like automated fortune-tellers. By 1910, these were joined by the bowling game Skee-Ball, and in the 1930s, the first coin-operated pinball machines started appearing.

Pinball was the king of games for decades. Arcades would have walls full of them—flashing, clanging, blaring music and "tilt" alarms. By the 1970s, pinball machines even ran on the same sophisticated technology that video games were being built with. Parts that used to be electromechanical (that is, made to move by mechanical gears powered with electricity) were replaced with light-up digital displays and the solid-state electronics of computers (a circuit board with microchips and no moving parts). But pinball wouldn't stay on top for long.

If you walked into any bowling alley, pool hall, or bar in the middle of the 1970s—any place where people would hang out—you'd spot a couple of video games against the side wall...usually made by Atari. Nolan Bushnell revisited his idea to make a driving game and produced *Gran Trak 10* in 1974. It featured an overhead view of a racetrack (drawn with white dots on a black screen), and the cabinet was mounted with a steering

wheel, gearshift, and pedals to acceler-
ate and brake. *Night Driver*, also from
Atari, took it a step further in 1976;
its whole game cabinet was a cockpit
for the player to sit in and drive from
a first-person point of view—the first
modern driving game. And Steve Jobs
and Steve Wozniak, who would later

Gran Trak 10

go on to found Apple, delivered *Breakout* for Atari in 1976,
a kind of one-person *Pong* where the player batted a ball
off a moving paddle at the bottom of the screen to smash
bricks at the top.

Nolan Bushnell, who always had an eye for where his
business could grow next, made two big moves after
Night Driver and *Breakout* were released. His company
developed and released the Atari 2600 home video game
console; and after the 2600's first year of sales (more
on this in the next chapter), he left Atari to start a new
business in 1978, a restaurant and family entertainment
center called Chuck E. Cheese's Pizza Time Theatre.
It combined a restaurant, animated entertainment (the
robotic performers of the Chuck E. Cheese band), and
a video game arcade. Bushnell's idea was to create a
place where the whole family could spend time out

together, as well as, conveniently, a venue to install his video games. He stocked his restaurant with a basic kitchen and decided to serve mainly pizza and french fries, which he determined were the easiest and cheapest foods to crank out. Bushnell's original Chuck E. Cheese restaurant, in San Jose, California, quickly became a series of franchise locations throughout the western United States, and today it's a worldwide chain. More importantly, Bushnell created the concept of the family entertainment center and of an arcade dedicated mainly to video games rather than pinball machines.

JAPAN CHANGES THE GAME

Taito, the Japanese company that launched its *Elepong* game earlier in the decade, was about to revolutionize everything. Tomohiro Nishikado, a young designer, had created several uninspired but successful games like *Soccer* for Taito, but he

Tomohiro Nishikado

wanted to create a new type of shooting game. As a kid, Nishikado had been a big fan of *The War of the Worlds*, a book by H.G. Wells, where tentacled Martians invaded Earth. He put together the idea of bug-like aliens with a concept he'd already been toying with, a game to shoot down airplanes. Drawing up the simplest, most identifiable pixelated creatures he could, he came up with the gameplay of rows of aliens descending on the screen, and Earth's only defense was a single missile launcher moving across the bottom...a bit like the paddle in *Breakout*. Like the very best video games, it was simple to play but extremely difficult to beat. The year was 1978. Nishikado called his game *Space Invaders*.

Was it a hit? Let's put it this way: in Japan, arcade games cost 100 yen. Popping in a 100-yen coin, like the American quarter, bought you a game. After *Space Invaders* was released, 100-yen coins disappeared from circulation all over Japan. So many people were pouring 100 yen into *Space Invaders* that it caused a nationwide shortage of the coins. The national bank of Japan even investigated the Taito company to make sure *Space Invaders* wasn't some kind of scam to stockpile the country's entire supply of 100-yen coins.

Nishikado also pioneered a new kind of video game cabinet; rather than the upright machines of before, he designed *Space Invaders* to be played on a table, with the screen laid horizontally in the top. Customers could sit and hunch over the table, staring down into it, with a place to put their pizza and soda while they played; game makers started calling this model of cabinet the "cocktail table."

Eventually *Space Invaders* also became an upright cabinet, and for much of the '80s, many of the classic video games would be built in both configurations, for standing or seated play. Taito sold 100,000 *Space Invaders* cabinets all over Japan, while in the United States, Bally Midway sold another 60,000. No other video game had ever come close.

THE COLOR BOOM

Just as *Spacewar!* inspired Bushnell's *Computer Space* and the gameplay of *Breakout* gave Nishikado an idea for *Space Invaders*, each generation of new video games inspired the ones to follow. *Space Invaders* inspired a follow-up game a year later by Namco, another Japanese company. *Galaxian* was extremely similar to its inspiration—a spaceship on a black screen fending off an attack wave of creepy creatures—but it amped up the difficulty by moving faster, removing the shields that protected the player at the bottom of the screen, and having its aliens swoop down to attack. But more notably, *Galaxian* added something no video game had featured before: color. In an arcade full of black screens and white shapes, *Galaxian* jumped out. Its terrifying bad guys were flying space insects in green, purple, red, and blue. Death meant the player's spaceship going up in a beautiful, brilliant explosion of yellow and red. *Galaxian*, released in 1979—and its 1981 sequel, *Galaga*—kicked open the doors for all the flashing colors that would fill arcades in the 1980s.

Galaxian

PAC-MAN FEVER

It's possible that no game was more iconic in its use of color than *Pac-Man*; but then, *Pac-Man* rightfully became a classic and legendary game because it pioneered a lot of firsts. It was the first game with a recognizable, charismatic lead character that players knew by name, instead of the nameless, never-seen heroes of *Space Invaders* and *Galaxian*. It also featured equally charm-

ing bad guys: the ghosts named Inky, Pinky, Blinky, and Clyde. No game before *Pac-Man* had ever had such catchy, memorable music and extremely unique

sound effects—anyone who's played *Pac-Man* at any length can hum the tune when a new level begins

and knows the sound of the hero chomping his way through the maze; the alarm-like blare when eating a

power pellet that makes your enemies turn blue; the bloop sound when you eat a ghost; and the heart-breaking but hilarious wail when Pac-Man dies. This was also the first game to launch a lucrative wave of tie-in merchandise like T-shirts, lunch boxes, stickers, and even a cartoon show—and this was by its creator's

design. It was also the first video game that successfully appealed to girls... also by design.

Toru Iwatani knew he wanted all of this when he set out to design a game for Namco. Because he knew that a face is a character's most memorable feature, he didn't just give his hero a face...he made his hero nothing but a face. When Iwatani's eye landed on a pizza with a single slice taken out, he envisioned a little round guy, chomping nonstop (who, in the English version, was originally called Puck-Man). He also reasoned that making the bad guys bright and colorful with huge, cute eyes would make them likable and popular...even when they killed you (*rew-rew-rew-rew—WAPWAP*). And he knew that making the sounds of the game as memorable as the visuals would double its power at bringing players back again and again. *Pac-Man*'s gameplay was really easy to learn, and extremely tough to beat. All you had to do was get through the maze, eat all the dots, and avoid those deadly ghosts. With the addition of the occasional piece of fruit floating through the maze for bonus points, a shortcut on each side of the screen that zipped you magically back to the opposite side, and power pellets to turn the tables and make Pac-Man deadly to the ghosts instead, the game's simple premise allowed for incredibly complex strategy.

Iwatani wanted his game to have broad appeal because he foresaw its potential for sales—not just the sale of addictive gameplay in exchange for quarters, but as a vehicle for merchandise. Even before pitching the game to his bosses at Namco, Iwatani personally mocked up some homemade T-shirts and sewed his own stuffed toys to give the company an idea of the possibilities. But *Pac-Man*'s success went beyond what even Iwatani had dreamed of; the game did successfully expand its appeal to girls and women, and the customer base for video games practically doubled. Arcades, which used to be filled mainly with boys, saw girls start to stream through the doors, and suddenly arcades became a place where couples could go on dates. *Pac-Man*, just by itself, generated so much business for arcades that it caused more of them to go into business all across the United States. It spawned multiple re-editions, sequels, and spin-offs, including *Ms. Pac-Man*, *Jr. Pac-Man*, *Super Pac-Man*, *Pac & Pal*, and *Pac-Man & Chomp-Chomp*, and it remains a hugely popular and beloved force of pop culture to this day.

Ms. Pac-Man

Jr. Pac-Man

Super Pac-Man

Pac-Man's Pal

Chomp-Chomp

SAVE THE SPACEMEN

Ironically, when *Pac-Man* made its debut for arcade industry professionals at a trade show in Chicago in October of 1980, it didn't make a splash. The game's U.S. distributor, Bally Midway—the same company that passed on *Pong*—didn't think a maze game would be very popular and didn't have very high expectations for the deal. But it had already agreed to distribute *Pac-Man*, and the game's monstrous success would come as a huge and positive surprise.

Eugene Jarvis

Another game, *Defender*, debuted at the same show; it didn't make a splash, either, but it would also go on to defy expectations and become a huge hit. Eugene Jarvis wanted to design pinball games, but by the time he started working, those were on their way out. He switched to video games reluctantly, intent on making a game as exciting and overwhelming as the chaotic action of a pinball machine. In the process, he also identified something other games were missing, and he built his game around it. Other games were about hostility and self-preservation—kill the bad guy and keep yourself alive—but as the title implies, *Defender* was about protecting others.

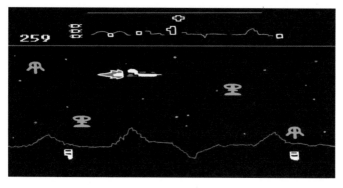

Defender

Like *Computer Space* and *Galaxian*, *Defender* featured a spaceship flying across a black screen; like *Space Invaders*, hostile aliens descended upon the planet below.

The new wrinkle? A crew of astronauts explored the surface on foot, and the aliens tried to abduct them. Astronauts who were abducted came back (presumably after grisly alien experiments) as mutant bad guys. When you fired at an alien abducting an astronaut, you could hit the astronaut if you weren't careful. And you had to be sure to catch any falling astronauts and lower them to the surface or they went splat. And it all happened fast. You can find video of *Defender*'s gameplay on YouTube; just watching it will make you break into a sweat. It was stressful; people loved it.

Missile Command was another arcade game that players found as compelling as they did stressful, but for very different reasons. In a down-to-earth twist on *Space Invaders*, 1980's *Missile Command* was set in a realistic city, shooting down nuclear missiles rather than alien bugs—harking back to the birth of video games as missile defense simulators for the U.S. military.

The year that *Pac-Man*, *Defender*, and *Missile Command* debuted in arcades, a young computer programmer named Dona Bailey was working at General Motors, helping to build dashboard displays and cruise control systems for cars. A friend took her to play *Space Invaders*, and Bailey was hooked on the arcade when she found out that Atari used the same microprocessors for games that she was trained in. In 1980, Dona Bailey became the first woman to join up with the coin-operated games department at Atari. Partnering with another developer named Ed Logg, Bailey cocreated *Centipede*, released in 1981, which pitted players against all manner of creepy crawlies, from scorpions and spiders to the titular creature working its way down the screen toward the player, in a clever update on the *Space Invaders* idiom.

Dona Bailey

Centipede was one of the greatest hits of Atari's arcade line. Bailey strove to make the game visually pleasing, in a color palette of fun greens and soothing pastels, even if the creatures onscreen were gross and unnerving. As one of the first and only women to contribute to the early history of video games, and the cocreator of a massive hit game, Bailey was a pioneer. This should have ensured the success and longevity of her career, but in spite of this, Dona Bailey left video games shortly after *Centipede,* joining a technology company in 1982 founded by two fellow ex-Atari employees. She had faced such intense pressure from her male colleagues and rivals within the industry that she turned her back on video games for over 25 years. Today, Dona Bailey is retired but makes public speaking appearances where she describes the early industry and encourages women and girls to pursue careers in video game creation.

A NEW PLAYER JOINS THE GAME

Atari, Taito, Namco, Bally Midway, even Williams —the company that staked its whole reputation on *Defender*—and others were enjoying success in video games. But one notable company hadn't appeared yet: Nintendo. It had the occasional modest hit in Japan, like the awkwardly translated *Laser Clay Shooting System* in 1973, a game designed around a revolutionary toy "zapper" made by the company's on-staff tinkerer, Gunpei Yokoi, that projected a beam of light. But Nintendo was languishing; it wanted to export a game to the United States and get in on the action. The company's most popular game was *Radar Scope*, another take on *Space Invaders*—this one with the aliens retreating to safety at the top of the screen and the added challenge of the hero's blaster getting slower the more it was fired. *Radar Scope* was a hit in Japan, and naturally, the company tried to follow up its success with several other games: *Space Firebird*, *Space Fever*, *Space Launcher*, each one was as indistinct as their repetitive titles suggest, copying earlier, more popular games. With little other choice, the president of Nintendo, Hiroshi Yamauchi, decided to try and export the successful *Radar Scope* to the United States.

It failed.

Toy "zapper" light gun

Yamauchi had hired his son-in-law Minoru Arakawa to head up Nintendo's new division, Nintendo of America, and sent him to the United States with 3,000 *Radar Scope* machines. Only about a thousand ended up in arcades, thanks to Arakawa's tireless hustle and salesmanship; the other 2,000 sat in a warehouse in New Jersey, gathering dust.

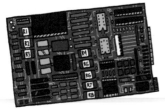

Arcade machine printed circuit board (PCB)

Nintendo was going to take a bath on video games, so to speak. The *Radar Scope* debacle was costing a fortune, and Yamauchi was desperate to figure out how that warehouse full of 2,000 cabinets could turn a profit, any way possible. The most practical idea still sounds incredibly far-fetched—Yamauchi could assign a programmer to rewrite the code on the *Radar Scope* microchip, reprogramming it into a totally new and different game. The outside of the cabinets could be redecorated with art for whatever the new idea was, and then Nintendo could see if it had better luck selling that one. Yamauchi turned to an unlikely candidate: Shigeru Miyamoto.

THE FATHER OF MARIO

Shigeru Miyamoto came to Nintendo
after studying industrial design; his father
had asked his friend Hiroshi Yamauchi
if there might be a job at Nintendo
for the young man. Miyamoto went

Shigeru Miyamoto

to work designing packaging art, painting cabinets,
and making up toys. When Yamauchi found himself in
trouble with the unsold *Radar Scope* units, he didn't
want to pull any of his professional programmers
from their important projects to come up with a new
game; instead, he put out an open call for Nintendo
employees to suggest ideas. Miyamoto, 29 years old,
came through with several. Yamauchi decided to
partner Miyamoto with his veteran tinkerer, Gunpei
Yokoi, to guide the younger man, as well as keep him
in line, just in case. And Yamauchi gave them one
directive: Nintendo was working on a licensing deal
for the comic-strip and cartoon character Popeye, so
Miyamoto and Yokoi should design a Popeye game.

That deal didn't end up coming together, but it gave
Miyamoto the idea for the characters he wanted:

a clever good guy like Popeye; his girlfriend, a wilting young woman like Olive Oyl; and a hulking, muscular bully like Bluto to kidnap her. This would instantly set up the conflict and give the underdog hero a mission. From there on out, Miyamoto designed a whole game by straining against his limitations, but working within the constraints of what the existing *Radar Scope* microchip and the controls on the cabinet could do. There was only a joystick and one button on the original game, for the spaceship to shoot at aliens, so Miyamoto thought about what one action a player could perform to move through a game. What he came up with seems basic, but it was something video game characters had never done before: jumping.

Miyamoto's original Mario design

Sitting down with a piece of graph paper, he designed his characters, filling in one square for each pixel. Miyamoto was limited to just three colors per character, so he used peach for the skin of the hero's face and hands, blue for his shoes and hair (black would have disappeared against the black background), and red for his clothes.

There wasn't even another color to give him a separate shirt, so Miyamoto made the hero's entire outfit red, using more blue for his arms so they would show against the body, and adding buttons to the chest, so the outfit would pass for overalls. Finally, he knew he didn't have enough pixels to draw good hair or a mouth, so Miyamoto covered the top of the hero's head with a

PIXELS AND SPRITES

When we talk about video game graphics, especially in these early years, we mostly talk about pixels and sprites.

Pixels are the individual dots of single color that combine to make the full multicolor image onscreen. When computers were rudimentary and video games were in their infancy, the fanciest of pixels were still big and blocky. As computer memory grew bigger and processing power got faster, pixels got smaller, and more of them fit on the screen. The smaller and more numerous pixels got, the more detailed graphics became.

The word "sprite" has a broader definition, but in the context of early video games, sprites were animated characters and shapes that moved independently of the game's static background. The hero the player controlled, for example, was a sprite, along with the bad guy they fought against and any objects like barrels that they threw at each other.

red hat and used more blue to give him a moustache, just to show where the mouth would be. You probably recognize this character by now, and you can see where this is going; Miyamoto named his jumping hero... Jumpman. (It was only after Miyamoto's game became a huge runaway success that they gave this hero his famous name—Mario.) The game Miyamoto was creating? *Donkey Kong.*

Jumpman (Mario) The Lady (Pauline) Donkey Kong

For visual contrast, Miyamoto designed the three characters to be different sizes; Mario's girlfriend, whom Miyamoto originally just called "the Lady," was twice as tall as the squat little Mario, and the villain (and title character) was even bigger than that. Donkey Kong was a giant, menacing gorilla with a muscular chest and a cartoonish, grinning face. Grabbing up the Lady (later renamed Pauline), he carried her to the top of a construction site and, jumping up and down, caused the girders to collapse.

Then he'd toss deadly barrels down the sloping girders as Mario climbed the half-constructed building, jumping over flaming oil drums and rolling barrels, to rescue Pauline.

The microchip was reprogrammed, and the prototype of the game was ready...now Nintendo just had to transform 2,000 *Radar Scopes* into 2,000 *Donkey Kongs* and sell them to arcades.

For the next several months, Nintendo of America swapped out and updated the circuit boards inside each *Radar Scope* cabinet and rebranded the outside with *Donkey Kong* art. As soon as they started shipping out the first few, they knew they had a hit. The game ended up selling 60,000 units in the United States, a success unheard of since *Space Invaders* and *Pac-Man*.

Donkey Kong

The game was an instant classic, and Nintendo finally joined the arcade revolution in a big way. *Donkey Kong* was, for starters, the first video game that ever had a story. Most of the people making video games were engineers, but Miyamoto had trained as an artist, and that's the way he approached this project. In spite of how many video games now existed, their styles of gameplay were limited to a handful of modes, designed from a standpoint of engineering: flying a spaceship, driving a car, hitting a ball, traversing a maze—basic functions of interactivity, with a game built around them. Shigeru Miyamoto started with ideas, characters, and relationships, and he let the mechanics of the game follow. He told a story by putting three characters in a situation of conflict (or, at least, two characters that take action, plus the damsel they repeatedly kidnap and rescue away from each other between levels). The hardy player who made it all the way to the end (an unbelievably difficult challenge) could see that story resolved; Mario rescues Pauline, and Donkey Kong falls off the building and lands on his head.

A basic rule of design—whether you're designing a phone, a power drill, a dress, or a video game—is that "form follows function." The object being designed must perform its function first, and then the form you design for it should serve that usefulness. When William Higinbotham designed *Tennis for Two*, the function of that game was to demonstrate the computer's ability to simulate gravity and wind resistance; the form it took in order to do that was a tennis match. As a designer, Miyamoto's idea for the function of *Donkey Kong* was to tell a story, first and foremost; everything else he worked with, from the use of the jump button to the look of the characters, was in service of that function.

By freeing up his thinking to approach a story in a new way, Miyamoto ended up creating an entirely new mode of gameplay—advancing through a barrage of obstacles to cross the space of the screen, jumping from platform to platform. Soon people started calling this kind of game a "platformer." And now that *Donkey Kong* was a proven success, Nintendo trusted Miyamoto to design all its best games, starting with a sequel, *Donkey Kong Jr.*, and a spin-off, *Mario Bros.* (which introduced the world to Mario's brother, Luigi). Miyamoto would have plenty of other opportunities to innovate, as Nintendo began to develop its next big venture: a home console.

LET'S PLAY
AT HOME

Video games enter the home, but the trip won't be easy; the leader in the field stumbles, and another player takes the controls.

The Legend of Zelda, see page 73

Following the worldwide success of *Pong* in arcades,
the department store chain Sears approached Atari
about selling a home version. Repackaging the popular game into its own console, Atari and Sears started
selling *Home Pong*; it plugged into your living room TV
set and came packaged with knob controllers, like the
original *Tennis for Two* gamepad and the controllers of
the Magnavox Odyssey. But with only one game playable on it, it was a costly investment. If families were
going to spring for an expensive home-gaming appliance,

it should provide more varieties of entertainment. In 1973, Atari was flush with cash from its first successful arcade games and eager to develop revolutionary new hardware. To invest in this development, the company bought Cyan Engineering, a small but promising research-and-development firm, and put it to the task of developing new video game systems. Atari/ Cyan's lead project was code-named Stella, a new kind of video game computer that would run whatever code was plugged into it, rather than depending on its own preprogrammed hard drive (the way that the Magnavox Odyssey, for example, could only play the games that came built in).

Nolan Bushnell knew this project would cost way more money than Atari had on hand and that it would need to happen fast or they'd get beaten to market by a better product from someone else. To secure a vast source of financing, Bushnell sold Atari in 1976 to Warner Communications, one of America's largest entertainment companies. The deal with Warner allowed Atari to pocket $28 million in the sale and gave it access to Warner's huge budgets. Together they poured $100 million of development funds into the Stella project.

A year later, the investment paid off, and the company released the Atari 2600 in 1977. It wasn't the first video game console with swappable cartridges, allowing players to collect a library of separate games and pop in whichever they felt like playing—that distinction belonged to an otherwise unremarkable console called the Fairchild Channel F. But even though Bushnell's product came in second he still won by launching a superior product and selling it better—just like he'd done with *Computer Space* six years earlier.

The 2600 was a revolutionary console, with more and better games than the competition; a sleek, wood-paneled design; and a

Atari 2600

streamlined, intuitive controller incorporating the familiar joystick-and-button playability of the arcades. Still, sales of the console were slightly disappointing that first year, which prompted a restless Bushnell to leave the company in 1978 and start his chain of arcades/pizza restaurants, Chuck E. Cheese's. But within a year, Atari realized it had cultivated a greater success than it had expected; the 2600 was expected to sell for only a couple of years, but by making the games a separate

A CUTTING-EDGE BUSINESS

Gillette was founded in 1901 to sell shaving razors. At the time, people shaved with a straight blade that had to be resharpened continually or with the newfangled invention of safety razors, handles with disposable all-purpose blades.

King Gillette (yes, his real name) got the idea to make custom, disposable blades that only worked with his patented razor and to sell those blades separately. He pioneered a business model where customers who bought one item, the razor, would keep coming back to buy a continuous supply of the blades to use with it—after all, why sell a product just once when you could sell replacements forever? In the spirit of King Gillette, Atari discovered that once customers had a 2600 console at home, they'd keep buying new games to play on it.

product, the company had stumbled onto something very lucrative. Businesspeople call it the "Gillette model" or the "razor and blades model" of sales; sell the customer one product—the console—and then keep them coming back again and again to buy the games.

Atari lured customers with a wide selection of the games they already loved playing at the arcade: *Pong*,

Space Invaders, Missile Command, Pac-Man, and many more. It also started to sign licensing deals with movie studios to base games on hit movies like *Star Wars, Raiders of the Lost Ark*, and *E.T.*

By then, it wasn't the only console in the business; during the years of Atari's greatest success with the 2600, the market was full of competitors, both good and bad. The toy company Mattel had scored a hit with its Intellivision, while Bally Midway had launched the Bally Astrocade to low sales. Coleco, another toy company, ensured the success of its ColecoVision console by releasing the official home version of *Donkey Kong*, after Atari passed on Nintendo's exorbitant asking price. But Atari was still the undisputed champion, taking an 80 percent share of the video game market, like Pac-Man gobbling up so many power pellets. By the early 1980s, the Atari 2600 was a fixture in many living rooms around the world. It transformed the TV set from a device for users to consume passively into an interactive entertainment appliance.

Video game consoles were selling, and it wasn't only an American playing field. In Great Britain, the inventor and entrepreneur Clive Sinclair had become wealthy and famous with a line of widely used pocket calculators. He was constantly inventing, even though some of his products flopped. When he lost out on an opportunity to make computers for the British Broadcasting Corporation, he set out to beat them at their own game with a better, faster, cheaper computer of his own. He released the ZX Spectrum in 1982; it was meant to be an all-purpose home computer, but its greatest power was its programmability, which made it an ideal platform for games. Sinclair spawned a British video game industry single-handedly, opening the doors for developers to create nearly 1,500 original Spectrum games in the first two years and prompting over 500 video game design companies to go into business.

In Japan, the successful arcade game maker Sega tried to join this booming business, with disappointing results. Sega was already a smash at arcades, with one of its most popular games taking Atari's *Night Driver* a step further. Rather than a racecar-driving game with a steering wheel on the console, Sega's *Hang-On* was a motorcycle game played while on a full-sized motorcycle simulator; the player sat astride an artificial motorcycle, steered it with the handlebars, and leaned to the side to make the bike turn in the game. Sega invested the profits from its hit arcade games into designing a home console, but it only produced the lackluster Sega SG1000. It was its first attempt, however, and learning from its failure, Sega would have better luck with the Sega Master System and even better luck with the Sega Genesis.

Sega Genesis

Despite kicking off a console revolution with the 2600—or, in fact, because of it—Atari suffered when the video game market became totally saturated by the early 1980s. Computers like the Commodore 64 in the United States, the ZX Spectrum in Europe, and the MSX in Japan were doing double duty as video game consoles, crowding into a field already jammed full with consoles. Even store chains had their own brands of consoles like the Sears Tele-Games and the Radio Shack Tandyvision. In the midst of this video game glut, Atari doubled down on the early success of its games by releasing more and more of them, faster and faster, with less and less care given to good design and good gameplay. To put it briefly, there were too many consoles, there were too many games, most of the games weren't very good, and there weren't enough buyers.

Atari, which had been the fastest-growing company in American history, saw its sales drop off a cliff. Desperate for a spike, it put another 10 million Atari 2600s into production...but anybody who was likely to buy a 2600 already had one. Then, hoping to recapture the appeal of a new console, the company rushed out the "new-and-improved" Atari 5200 in 1982...a dressed-up version of the 2600 that was not actually new, was barely improved, and had an all-too-complicated controller covered in numbered buttons. It barely sold. The company lost a fortune, and in 1984, Warner sold off Atari. Under new management and with a tweaked name, Atari Corporation would go on to be a forgettable also-ran in the console wars between Nintendo and Sega for the next 15 years. This was the end of an era.

THE FAMILY COMPUTER

What Atari had done by accident—stumbling into the Gillette model—Hiroshi Yamauchi wanted Nintendo to do on purpose. When the company president pitched Nintendo's own video game console, the Famicom, to salespeople in Japan in 1983, he told them not to expect profits on the costly machine but on the games instead. Still, the Famicom was going to be a tough sell. The collapse of the video game market hadn't really affected Japan, so Yamauchi saw an opportunity to fill the vacuum with the console his company had slowly been developing for years. But he knew selling it to the United States would be much harder.

Nintendo's talented tinkerer, Gunpei Yokoi, repaired playing card machines and occasionally invented toys like the telescoping fake hand. One day, when Yokoi was assigned to chauffeur Yamauchi's luxury car, the inventor told his boss about an idea he had—simple games played on LCD screens (like digital watches) that could be made cheaply, run on a watch battery, and be sold as portable video games. Yamauchi liked the idea, and Nintendo manufactured it as the Game & Watch. The company's first game was a juggling game called *Ball* in 1980. More notably, Yokoi made some of the Game & Watch games playable with a new design of controller that would eventually change everything—the "D-pad." Joysticks were prone to break, especially on a cheap, portable device, but flattening the joystick into a four-arrow directional pad was cheap to produce, easy to use, and durable...plus it looked cool.

Game & Watch

By the time Yamauchi saw an opportunity to expand Nintendo's home gaming division into consoles, he had appointed Gunpei Yokoi to lead the company's first games research-and-development division, which they called R&D1. Even before Shigeru Miyamoto had begun work on *Donkey Kong* years earlier, Yamauchi could see that home video game computers would be a valuable opportunity in the future, and he had set R&D1 the task of quietly developing a console and games. Yamauchi knew that the most reliable path to success involved careful planning and preparation, and he knew that Nintendo's console would need to be as well designed as possible, with a wide variety of games available upon release. He also knew that once retailers considered consoles poisonous, he'd need to find another angle.

Nintendo Famicon

The Nintendo Famicom (short for Family Computer) was designed to look like a toy—white and red with rounded edges, instead of sleek, sharp, and dark like the consoles that came before it—and it showed off Nintendo's characteristic inventiveness. The player-2 controller came with a built-in microphone, and the console was equipped with modem compatibility. It's a testament to Nintendo's foresight that a console released in 1983 was designed to work with a modem, at a time when most families didn't even have home computers, let alone the internet. What's more, the company had the technology to power its first console with a 16-bit microchip—the kind of chip that

HIROSHI YAMAUCHI

Fusajiro Yamauchi founded the Marufuku playing card company in 1889 and sold his products in a store he called Nintendo Koppai. When he retired, he handed control of the company to his grandson, Hiroshi Yamauchi, at the very young age of 21.

The younger Yamauchi tried to expand the family business by branching out into any opportunity he saw—instant rice, toys, taxicabs, and even discreet hotels for lovers to meet secretly—but nothing was really working.

When Yamauchi saw how well electromechanical games and video games were doing in Japan in the early 1970s, he believed his company, now officially renamed Nintendo, might have a future in video games.

would make graphics really slick and advanced—but it elected to stick with 8-bit, which would be more affordable for Nintendo to produce and would allow it to keep the sale price lower for customers.

To play the Famicom, the R&D1 team envisioned the first controller that would be operated with both hands rather than held in one and played with the other, like the Atari's joystick. They incorporated Gunpei Yokoi's inspired design of the D-pad and action buttons from the *Donkey Kong* Game & Watch and opted for two action buttons under the right thumb—enough for a variety of gameplay functions, but basic enough to limit developers to keep their games simple and intuitive. This would be the standard gamepad for the next 15 years, replicated on the Game Boy, Super NES, Sega Genesis, and more.

Nintendo released the Famicom in Japan in 1983, in the wake of Atari's meltdown, and it became an instant smash. Gunpei Yokoi's team—and their rising superstar Shigeru Miyamoto—had come up with instant Nintendo classics like *Metroid* and *Kid Icarus* for the Famicom. But Miyamoto's prowess at spearheading inventive games like *Donkey Kong* and *Excitebike* (a side-scrolling dirt-bike racing game that incorporated turbo boosters and an overheating bike) earned him a promotion. Before Nintendo took its console to America, Yamauchi knew he would need the best games; he opened a new development division, R&D4, and he put Miyamoto in charge.

MARIO GETS SUPER

Shigeru Miyamoto had invented the single-screen platformer in *Donkey Kong* and modified that into a two-player head-to-head with *Mario Bros.*, as Mario and Luigi spar in a good-natured fight to win coins. Seeking to expand on the platform concept, Miyamoto's next design for arcades and the Famicom was a game called *Ice Climber*, where you not only had to go up the platforms, but the screen scrolled upward as you did. It introduced the bottom of the screen as a new obstacle—getting caught down there would cost you a life—and moved the gameplay experience in a vertical direction. Now Miyamoto was tasked with designing a launch game for the U.S. debut of the Nintendo Entertainment System, and by now Nintendo had embraced

Mario as its star and mascot, showcasing him in half a dozen different games for arcades, Famicom, and Game & Watch. Miyamoto would design a signature NES game to star Mario.

It is impossible to overstate the importance of Shigeru Miyamoto's next creation. *Super Mario Bros.* may well be the most famous video game of all time, or the most influential, or the most beloved...or likely, all of the above. The game sold more than 40 million copies around the world, and it remained the world's highest-selling video game for 20 years after its launch.

As always, Miyamoto started with his story. Mario, the everyday working man, would enter a bizarre and unfamiliar kingdom and embark on a kind of knight's quest to vanquish a monster (the reptilian Bowser) and rescue a damsel (Princess Toadstool), an adventure seemingly far above his station as a humble plumber. Players, many of whom were young and relatively unaccustomed

to video games before getting their first Nintendo, could relate to the fish-out-of-water feeling of entering such a weird and confusing world. From that standpoint, every new surprise and discovery the game threw at players— coins hidden inside bricks, strange mushroom creatures, secret warp zones, invincibility stars, bad guys tossing spiny animals from a flying cloud—only served to enhance the game's wonder and delight.

Once the overall idea was in place, Miyamoto began to tinker with the moving parts—how to make the game work. Games like *Defender* had already experimented with gameplay extending beyond the edges of the screen and scrolling back and forth to cover it, but Miyamoto combined that concept with the continuous upward movement of his *Ice Climber* game, shifted in a new direction, to create steady, left-to-right forward progress. The player can't go backward once the screen has crossed a point, and the question of what will appear next as the game scrolls to the right is a constant source of anticipation and suspense. With *Donkey Kong* Miyamoto created the platformer; now he was inventing the genre of game that would come to be called the "side scroller."

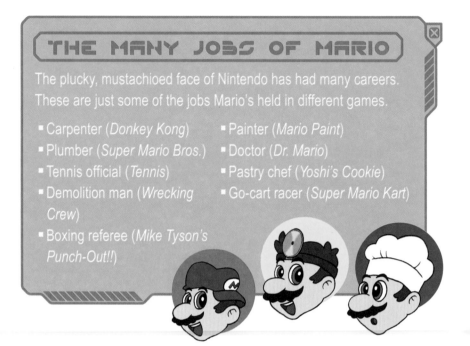

THE MANY JOBS OF MARIO

The plucky, mustachioed face of Nintendo has had many careers. These are just some of the jobs Mario's held in different games.

- Carpenter (*Donkey Kong*)
- Plumber (*Super Mario Bros.*)
- Tennis official (*Tennis*)
- Demolition man (*Wrecking Crew*)
- Boxing referee (*Mike Tyson's Punch-Out!!*)
- Painter (*Mario Paint*)
- Doctor (*Dr. Mario*)
- Pastry chef (*Yoshi's Cookie*)
- Go-cart racer (*Super Mario Kart*)

Super Mario Bros. became such a smash in Japan that Nintendo started packaging it with new shipments of the Famicom. In the West, it became the launch game that came with the Nintendo Entertainment System when the console first debuted in the U.S. and in Europe in 1986.

Minoru Arakawa, the president of Nintendo of America, faced an uphill climb to convince U.S. stores to carry the NES. Retailers who had been stuck with unsold Atari 2600s, ColecoVisions, and every other console under the sun were not interested in stocking another one.

But Arakawa offered store owners an irresistible deal—
Nintendo would *give* stores the NES for 90 days, then
the stores could pay Nintendo for whatever they sold
and return any inventory left over, if they wanted to.
It was a safe bet for store owners, so they stocked the
NES confidently; they were rewarded by selling 50,000
NES consoles in only three months and another million
by the first year. Nintendo captured 90 percent of the
entire video game market by 1990.

Designing *Donkey Kong*, single-handedly ensuring
Nintendo's success, and completely revolutionizing the
video game industry was a feat for Shigeru Miyamoto
and the kind of achievement that would seem impossible to repeat. When he designed *Super Mario Bros.*,
he did it again. A year later, he would do it yet again.

A LIVING LEGEND

For years, Miyamoto had approached each design challenge from new perspectives to keep the experience
fresh for himself and for players, orienting gameplay in
new directions—platform-climbing movement within a
stationary screen, a screen scrolling upward in a contin-

uous climb, and a world scrolling sideways like the unfurl-ing of a scroll. For his next game, Miyamoto wanted to recapture his childhood experiences of wandering freely and exploring the countryside outside the city of Kyoto.

Miyamoto was used to building his stories around levels, narrative progression, and boss battles (battles against significant opponents at the end of levels or games), all of which ran counter to the free-form exploratory ap-peal of the fantasy role-playing genre that was popular in Japan. Hiroshi Yamauchi wasn't especially a fan of those games, either. But Japan's version of the Famicom had a built-in disk drive, and the Nintendo president thought they could take advantage of its capabilities for memory to create a larger game, expanding in every direction beyond the simple platformers and side scrollers the com-pany had been able to fit in a cartridge so far.

Given that directive from the boss, Miyamoto set out to build a vast world that the player was free to roam through...but also to wrangle it into the familiar narra-tive flow of chapter-like levels and bosses. He designed an ecosystem of forests, deserts, lakes, rivers, graveyards, mountains, waterfalls, and hidden underground dungeons.

And to give the player the most expansive view possible of this sprawling world—the kingdom of Hyrule—Miyamoto devised yet another fresh viewpoint: straight overhead. The player could wander freely in any direction on the map, and Miyamoto created a sense of progression

Link

by demarcating the hero's progress through his achievements. He named his hero Link, a brave young boy in a green tunic and hat. This was *The Legend of Zelda*.

At the start of the game, Link has no sword and only a weak wooden shield; he meets an old man who gives him a simple sword made of wood—"It's dangerous to go alone! Take this." As Link discovers one hidden dungeon after another, explores their depths, and defeats the monsters locked within, he gathers more weapons and tools, grows stronger, and even changes clothes. By the end of the game, the boy who started out with a green tunic and a wooden sword now wears a red tunic; he carries a boomerang, bow and arrow, bombs, magic wand, health potions, and more; and he wields the mighty Master Sword. Link quests to defeat the evil sorcerer Ganon, recover the shattered pieces of the mythical Triforce, and rescue Princess Zelda.

There was only one problem: in Japan, the Famicom had the built-in disk drive to store all this information, but the NES did not. *Zelda* was too big to play in one sitting; for the first time ever, thanks to the Famicom's memory, players could save their game, turn off the console, and come back later to keep working on it. Without the disk drive for saving, NES players would never be able to explore Hyrule. But Nintendo knew it had a massive hit on its hands, so it spared no expense; the NES version of *Zelda* was manufactured with an extra memory card inside the cartridge to store the saved information, and to power the memory card, it had its own built-in battery.

Ten years earlier, Atari had wielded such mastery over the video game industry that it became a victim of its own success, believing it could do no wrong, saturating the market, diluting the quality of its games, and inspiring a wave of imitators. Nintendo, through patience, good timing, hard work, and luck, was avoiding all of those traps. It virtually owned the video game business of the 1980s and was unopposed. But that didn't mean contenders weren't eyeballing its success.

Sega, the company that flopped with the SG1000, took its lumps and went back to work. Hideki Sato, the same engineer who had directed Sega's development division

Sega Mark III

called the Away Team to create the SG1000, led the project to create the Sega Mark III. Sato studied the Famicom carefully and tried to figure out every way he could build a device that was stronger, faster, and cooler looking. Sega expanded its operation to the United States for the first time, opening a sales office with two American employees, Bob Harris and Bruce Lowry. They renamed their console the Sega Master System and released it two years after the Famicom, in 1985. It wasn't a hit—in fact, it was barely a blip in Nintendo's rearview—but some players maintain that it was better than the NES. Sega was learning...and it would come back a third time, stronger than ever.

THE SUPER NINTENDO VS. SEGA GENESIS

SLUGFEST

"**S**uper Nintendo, Sega Genesis / when I was dead broke, man, I couldn't picture this." —Notorious B.I.G.

As video games get faster, brighter, louder, and bloodier, the pressure to compete turns into all-out war.

Mortal Kombat; see page 87

The 1990s were an explosive moment for popular culture. As cable television became common, the average American household went from having three broadcast networks and a couple of local TV stations, transmitted by antenna, to 50 or 60 channels wired in at high definition. Almost overnight, the airwaves were filled with programming that competed more and more aggressively to win viewers' attention. In the fight for ratings, and with fewer restrictions on cable TV content, shows used every card in the deck: violence, nudity, drug use, and all other manner of shock value. Of course, this isn't to say it was all bad; cable TV became fertile ground for innovative, revolutionary programming, and it sparked a cultural boom that improved the quality of television forever.

Nevertheless, it was a battleground, and video games had to fight, too. In a world of fast-paced, rapid-fire, violent entertainment, the staid, slow-paced video games of the past no longer held as much appeal for a jaded youth. *Donkey Kong* and *Pac-Man* were nostalgia—still beloved, a charming curiosity from years ago, but hardly the phenomenon they had been a decade before. Arcades were losing business as more kids stayed home to play on consoles and watch cable TV. Mario and Luigi were cultural institutions, and their games still sold in record numbers, but they were ready for a shake-up. And they'd get one.

Nintendo had reached the limits of innovation with the 8-bit NES. If it wanted to continue creating new and unprecedented game design, the hardware had to evolve. To that end, Nintendo had been patiently developing a second-generation console. Sixteen-bit microchips were now more affordable than when Nintendo had originally considered powering the NES with one, and that would be the basis of its new machine—the Super Famicom, a.k.a. the Super NES. But the company was beaten to market by an unexpected competitor.

Super Famicon

After the paltry success of the Master System in 1985, Sega went into overdrive. Hayao Nakayama, the president of Sega Enterprises in Japan, ordered the development of a new console, one powerful enough to adapt Sega's successful arcade games faithfully. He aspired to launch the world's first 16-bit system, and he did—the Sega Mega Drive was released in Japan in 1988. It sold better than the Master System, but it still couldn't put a dent in Nintendo's uncontested popularity. So Nakayama imagined a more subversive way to take on Nintendo; he would move the fight from their home turf of Japan to a market where Sega might be able to mount a stronger challenge: the United States.

Sega Mega Drive

Tom Kalinske was an American toy executive with a gift for elevating products

Tom Kalinske

from has-beens and also-rans to serious contenders. As an executive at Mattel, he had been in charge of Barbie dolls, and he shepherded the doll line from its struggling perch as a holdover of the 1960s to a booming, multibillion-dollar business. After a fight with other Mattel executives over who would become the next president of the company, Kalinske left to run Matchbox, the washed-up toy car company that had consistently lost out to Mattel's Hot Wheels line. He whipped Matchbox into shape in no time at all, leading the company to growth and profits. Just when he was looking for his next chapter, he received a visit from Hayao Nakayama. Sega was overhauling its U.S. operation, and Nakayama personally recruited Kalinske as president and CEO of Sega of America. The job came with a simple mandate: import the Sega Mega Drive to the United States and sell a million of them. Going up against Nintendo was no small task, but Kalinske went right to work.

It was primarily a war waged through advertising. The Mega Drive,

Hayao Nakayama

renamed the Sega Genesis in the United States for copyright reasons, was immediately marketed as a more adult offering than Nintendo's system. Kalinske put out the Genesis in limited release in New York and Los Angeles, packaged with games like *Altered Beast*—a violent, bloody adventure starring a bare-chested muscleman brought back to life by Zeus and cursed to transform into different animalistic creatures as a power-up (with the memorable sound clip "Riiiise from your grave!")—and the sword-and-sorcery, hack-and-slash game *Golden Axe*, featuring a brawny barbarian and a scantily clad warrior vixen. Sega also boasted better sports games than anything by Nintendo, branded and endorsed by sports stars no less, such as *Tommy Lasorda Baseball* and *Joe Montana Football*.

The *Altered Beast* muscleman, transformed

Sega's U.S. advertising was tailored to antagonize Nintendo directly, portraying the bright and colorful NES games as "kids' stuff"—the kiss of death for a brash and in-your-face generation of teens—and to push the Genesis with the confrontational slogan "Sega does what

Nintendon't." These maneuvers worked; when the Sega Genesis arrived on American shores in 1989, the NES had been around for years. Sega didn't just erode Nintendo's market share in new sales, it completely took it away. As the holidays approached that first year, 90 percent of new video game consoles sold were the exciting Sega Genesis, vastly more appealing to customers than the familiar old NES.

But Sega still needed a face, a mascot. Hayao Nakayama challenged his designers in Japan to come up with a Mario of their own and a video game for the mascot to star in, which Sega could package in new shipments of the Genesis instead of *Altered Beast*. Nakayama's only stipulation was that the character should jump. Designers rejected a kangaroo or a bunny as too cutesy. They liked the idea of an armadillo, which could roll into a ball, creating a new dynamic of movement. Finally, based on an idea sketched out by Masato Oshima, an on-staff artist, Sega picked its mascot: a blue hedgehog. Tom Kalinske and the whole team at Sega of America hated it.

Taking all his cues from Mario, Yuji Naka, a proven

Sega designer, headed up a development outfit called Sonic Team to create the game—*Sonic the Hedgehog*, released in 1991. Naka limited all of *Sonic*'s controls to just the directional pad and one button for jumping—even simpler than Mario—and he kept elements that were familiar to players, like collecting coins (in *Sonic*'s case, gold rings), but rocketed everything up as fast as the game could possibly handle. Sonic moved so unbelievably fast that, if a player idled in one spot too long, the hedgehog would tap his foot impatiently and scowl directly at the viewer. Sonic was designed to be everything Mario was not; where Mario was jovial and chubby, Sonic was rude and covered in sharp, windswept points. Mario ambled through his games, occasionally jogging; Sonic pitched forward and raced at a non-stop breakneck pace. Mario wore uncool overalls; Sonic sported chunky red sneakers. Sonic was a stinker—Bugs Bunny with a mean attitude and an incessant need for speed. People loved him.

Fighting back against *Sonic the Hedgehog* and the Sega Genesis wouldn't be Nintendo's only challenge with the next-gen console it was developing. Barring the underwhelming, failed launch of consoles like the Atari 5200, this was the first time that a company had successfully sold millions of expensive consoles and now, less than a decade later, expected people to upgrade to a newer, better model. People who splurged on an NES for their kids assumed a video game console would be a one-time purchase; as in the Gillette model, it was one piece of expensive hardware that new games could be purchased for forever. They weren't happy to hear the NES was out of date and that kids were begging for a 16-bit Super NES now. Parents mounted a boycott before the new console even launched, and in turn, store owners refused to carry it, lest they get stuck with unsold inventory. Despite the proven success of the NES, Minoru Arakawa and Nintendo of America were forced to negotiate sweetheart deals with retailers: stock the Super NES free until you see proven sales, then pay on the back end and return unwanted inventory. Nintendo had faith in the quality of its product, and it was willing to bend over backwards to prove it. Much like the original launch of the NES, the Super NES was an instant hit, and Arakawa's cajoling for shelf space paid off for retailers and the company as units flew out of stores. Still, the allure of the new was a lot to contend with, and the Sega Genesis and *Sonic the Hedgehog* outsold the Super NES two to one in their first holiday season in direct competition. For the first time ever, the market of video game consoles was a head-to-head battle.

THE TWILIGHT OF ARCADES

Meanwhile, arcades were on life support. The quality of graphics, sound, and gameplay in the 16-bit home consoles had lapped the superior performance once expected from arcade games. If the old business model was going to survive, it would have to become as competitive as consoles and television had.

Street Fighter had been a somewhat popular arcade game from the Japanese developer Capcom, but in 1991 it was eclipsed by its immensely more popular sequel, *Street Fighter II*. The game's primary appeal was its cast of compelling characters—everyone from the somewhat conventional, like karate students Ryu and Ken and the American military man Guile, to the outlandish and bizarre, like the Brazilian monster-man Blanka and Dhalsim, a stereotypical Hindu ascetic—brought together by the criminal M. Bison for a tournament fought in interesting settings all over the world.

More than just street fighters, the characters had unusual powers and abilities. Ryu and Ken might have been a couple of ordinary dudes, but their mastery of karate extended to generating fireballs from thin air that they flung at opponents. Chun-Li was a particularly beloved and influential *Street Fighter II* character, but not an uncontroversial one, either. Although her outfit was a collection of feminine Chinese clichés, and the high slits in her skirt frequently revealed her underwear, she was nevertheless a formidable character. Chun-Li became a favorite of girls and women, arguably even more than of the teen boys who would make her throw high kicks over and over.

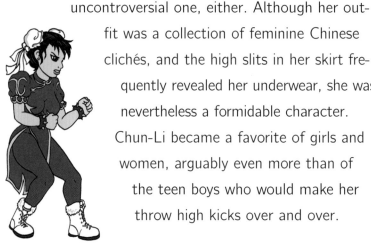

Chun-Li

Combining exciting characters, over-the-top fighting styles, animated backgrounds full of detail, fast action, and a wide variety of button combos for players to master in order to pull off each character's unique moves (down-down-forward-forward-punch..."Hadouken!"), *Street Fighter II* was a monster success. Arcades that had teetered on the brink of insolvency were kept in business and carried back to profitability by the addictive gameplay that kept bringing in customers for endless tournaments. And in spite of all its fighting violence and cultural insensitivity, it wasn't even that graphic of a game; there was no blood and no death. *Street Fighter II* was a cartoon.

Not so with *Mortal Kombat*. The other arcade fighting hit of the '90s—and in fact, the best-selling fighting franchise of the decade and of all time—became a smash through pure shock value. *Mortal Kombat*, released in 1992, also had signature character moves and hit combos. What *Mortal Kombat* featured that no other video game had was blood and gore—buckets of it. During the course of a match, the characters get progressively bloodier and more injured, and red puddles form on the ground around them. If the characters of *Street Fighter II* were cartoons, the fighters of *Mortal Kombat* came straight out of horror movies. Ed Boon,

Unfortunately, when *Donkey Kong* became the first video game to tell a story, it also set a precedent of female characters being underrepresented, underdeveloped, and stereotyped. The helpless **Pauline**, who was just a prize to be stolen away by Donkey Kong and won back by Mario, didn't even have a name at first; she was only "the Lady."

This trend sadly continues to a large extent today, as female characters are all too often reduced to a kidnapping victim to be rescued, or bait set by a villain to trap a hero, or otherwise victimized or objectified in multiple ways.

Mercifully there were always exceptions. Among the multiple possible endings of Nintendo's 1986 classic *Metroid*, one has the intergalactic bounty hunter Samus Aran removing bulky armor to reveal she was a woman all along, one of video games'

a video game developer, and John Tobias, a graphic designer and comic book artist, developed an idea for a fighting game starring the action movie star Jean-Claude Van Damme. When that didn't pan out, they turned their idea into a new concept in fantasy and horror. Fighters included Scorpion, who removed his mask to reveal a flame-breathing skull for a head; Sub-Zero,

first notable female heroes. And while characters like Chun-Li from the Capcom arcade game *Street Fighter II* (1991) and Lara Croft from *Tomb Raider* (released in 1996 for the Sega Saturn and Sony PlayStation) seemed like eye candy for men, they were strong, fighting women nevertheless.

Today, a new generation of young creators are developing more games with female protagonists than ever before, like 2017's *Horizon Zero Dawn* for the PlayStation 4. And critics like Anita Sarkeesian, a cultural commentator specializing in video games and pop culture, contribute to this ongoing discussion. Sarkeesian's series of web videos, *Tropes vs. Women in Video Games*, which ran on YouTube from 2013 to 2017, discussed the objectification and neglect of women and violence against female characters. The popular and widely respected *Tropes* web series made many eloquent, well-reasoned arguments, but Sarkeesian became the undeserving target of widespread online harassment for tackling these topics.

who could freeze an opponent with ice breath; the four-armed inhuman monster Goro; and Raiden, a kung fu master with lightning bolts sparking from his fingertips and eyes. A match held in a dungeon featured severed heads on spikes; when Goro defeated an opponent, he would rip the corpse in two. Most infamously, every match ended with "Finish him!"—when the winner was prompted by the game to execute a special move and kill their opponent as violently and graphically as possible. *Mortal Kombat* inspired outrage, protests, parental boycotts, and even a U.S. Senate inquiry into video game violence.

Led by these two blockbusters, the flagging arcade business attracted customers with the scope and spectacle

"E" FOR EVERYONE

With its inclination toward games more "grown-up" than Nintendo's "kid stuff," Sega occasionally found itself in hot water over the amount of violence in Genesis games. When *Mortal Kombat* came to the Genesis—along with other violent games like 1992's horror movie–themed *Splatterhouse 2*—Sega was motivated to create the Videogame Rating Council, which later inspired the creation of the Entertainment Software Rating Board. This independent organization grants classifications for all the games released by the industry, designating what specific players each game is suitable for.

- **EC**—Early Childhood
- **E**—Everyone
- **E10+**—Everyone over age 10

that home consoles couldn't provide. *Street Fighter II* and *Mortal Kombat* would both get ported to Super NES and Sega Genesis for home gameplay, but no television set could provide the crowd experience of friends and strangers watching and cheering a match over the players' shoulders. Arcade games like *X-Men* and *Teenage Mutant Ninja Turtles* (side scrollers) would raise the stakes even further by spreading their action across two or even four interconnected screens—depending on which version of the game an arcade owner was willing to invest in—allowing simultaneous gameplay by two, three, or four users.

The excesses of the '90s granted the arcade business a stay of execution, but not for long. Although family entertainment venues like Dave & Buster's still exist in the vein pioneered by Chuck E. Cheese's, with wall-to-wall rows of machines, the arcade of old is a dying breed. Video game cabinets have gone back to their pre-arcade niches—a handful of them against a side wall at the multiplex, at the pizzeria, or at the bowling alley.

GAME OVER FOR

NINTENDO?

The Nintendo/Sega race ends unceremoniously as Sega runs out of gas and Nintendo pulls ahead— into the perfect position to make the gravest miscalculation of its existence.

Tetris, played on home computers, in arcades, and on the Game Boy; designed by Alexey Pajitnov, 1984

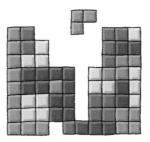

For all the difficulty that the Sega Genesis gave the Super NES, company turmoil inside Sega allowed sales of the console to slow down and fall behind. Nintendo and Sega both knew that games on disc were in the near future—a disc could hold much more information than a cartridge—and the time would come to double down on processing power again and graduate to a 32-bit system.

The Sega CD drive and the Sega 32X add-ons were

Sega's attempts to get ahead of this curve while it worked on developing its next console. But the accessories were costly, and fans considered them largely pointless. Meanwhile, Hayao Nakayama had directed his company's resources to develop a project code-named the Giga Drive. It was to be a 32-bit machine with sophisticated three-dimensional graphic rendering capabilities. And it would end up being an expensive system... priced for retail at nearly $400.

Sega's focus on this new project led the company to neglect the Sega Genesis. Even though sales were holding up well, the company slowed manufacturing and didn't produce enough consoles for the 1995 holiday season. This lag allowed Nintendo to take back more of the market share from Sega than it would have been able to otherwise, mainly with two surprise products.

Gunpei Yokoi, who had invented the Game & Watch with cheap technology that was already on its way out, updated that concept with one of Nintendo's most ingenious product launches in 1989: the Game Boy. This

Gunpei Yokoi

handheld console was designed to be as inexpensive as physically possible; all the components were virtually obsolete and thus cheap to buy and cheap to assemble. The technology to build a full-color, back-lit handheld device ex-

Game Boy

isted—Sega used it to launch the Game Gear in 1990, and even Atari tried to stay in the game with the Lynx, the handheld companion to its underperforming console, the Atari Jaguar—but Yokoi and Nintendo deliberately opted for a simple machine with a monochrome screen. The Game Boy's graphics weren't even black and white; they were plain black on a green screen that had no backlight, so you couldn't play it in the dark. All the sound came through one tinny speaker.

The upshot was that the Nintendo Game Boy only took four AA batteries, and they lasted a good amount of time, as opposed to the Sega Game Gear, which ate up six batteries in just a few hours. Even though the Game Gear was a fancier, slicker, edgier machine, the Game Boy outsold it consistently and started an entire prod-uct line of portable consoles for Nintendo, selling over 200 million units in its various forms.

With the Game Boy, Nintendo kicked off a fruitful era of handheld game consoles, for itself and its competitors. These are some of the most notable:

GAME BOY

The console that started it all in 1989. The Game Boy was inspired by the portability and affordability of Nintendo's own Game & Watch devices, updated with interchangeable cartridges.

GAME GEAR

Sega meant for its 1991 handheld to blow Game Boy out of the water, but it never quite did. Even with the Game Gear's superior technology and better graphics and sound, customers kept buying the cheaper device with longer battery life.

GAME BOY COLOR

The 1998 update to the Game Boy could play the original system's cartridges, along with a new generation of full-color games.

GAME BOY ADVANCE

Nintendo's 2001 follow-up to the Game Boy, with advanced graphics and sound and a wide selection of games, was a huge hit for the company.

NINTENDO DS

In 2004 Nintendo leveled up the Game Boy line again with the Nintendo DS (for dual screen), featuring a touchscreen with a stylus and a microphone you could speak and even blow into. Future iterations would even boast three-dimensional graphics.

PLAYSTATION PORTABLE

Sony's 2005 PSP device was a massive hit, thanks in large part to its interactivity with the PlayStation 2 and 3 and the power to play movies on mini-disc with cinema-quality picture and sound.

NINTENDO SWITCH

Nintendo's newest home console, released in 2017, doubles as its new handheld console, with a removable tablet and controllers that can be taken on the go.

Secondly, Nintendo was holding steady with the success of numerous Super NES games in its signature franchises: *Super Mario World*, *The Legend of Zelda: A Link to the Past*, and *Super Metroid* were all excellent games that gave players a faithful installment of the franchise while updating each one for a new generation. *A Link to the Past* in particular stands out as one of Super NES's finest games of all. *Super Mario Kart* introduced Mario and his cast of characters to a new setting, go-cart racing, with such success that it would launch an entirely new franchise with more than half a dozen sequels across as many consoles.

But the biggest hit of the Super NES's later years was as much of a surprise to Nintendo as to its fans; Nintendo enjoyed a new lease on life based on the success of just one game—a game that was such a smash, it buoyed the company's fortunes, allowed Nintendo to keep a toehold against not only Sega, but an unexpected new console competitor (more on this in a bit), and bought it time to fine-tune its next big launch. That game was called *Donkey Kong Country*.

Nintendo, Sega, and other players in the business all knew the future of video game graphics was three-dimensional rendering of its sprites—the animated characters who move across the screen. Instead of drawing characters as flat, two-dimensional pictures, the way they'd ultimately appear on the screen, 3-D rendering meant building them in special software as if they were digital sculptures; they could be tilted, spun, and viewed from any angle, and every detail would be there. Then these 3-D figures would get placed like action figures in the world of the game. But the computing muscle that it took for a video game cartridge to deliver 3-D sprites appeared to be out of reach for a 16-bit system. Until someone figured it out.

Tim & Chris Stamper

Brothers Tim and Chris Stamper were video game fans working in England who jumped at the opportunity provided by Clive Sinclair's ZX Spectrum computer to program their own video games in the early 1980s. They were eager to understand console gaming, and they reverse-engineered an NES, taking it apart to figure out how it worked. They founded a studio called Rare and began making games, becoming one of the most popular and successful development studios of the '80s and '90s. It wasn't long before they came to the attention of Nintendo.

In the '90s, the Stampers were experimenting with 3-D sprites rendered with expensive computers made by Silicon Graphics, hoping to produce a boxing game. Senior executives from Nintendo visited their workshop and saw their early development, reporting about it enthusiastically to Hiroshi Yamauchi. It was a degree of rendering and animation that had seemed impossible for 16-bit microprocessors, but here it was before their eyes. Nintendo bought a stake of Rare and brought the brothers aboard to build it a game. The Stampers asked for a crack at *Donkey Kong*, and they got it. It was the first time a *Donkey Kong* game wasn't made by Shigeru Miyamoto, although the gorilla's creator did review the game's progress and weigh in with his expert input, adding key elements and moves.

The Stampers'
Donkey Kong

The Stampers dressed Donkey Kong in a red necktie, like he'd worn in the Game Boy version from 1994, but their otherwise total redesign of the character became Nintendo's new standard, and it continues to be how Donkey Kong is represented today. This new iteration of Donkey Kong, and the world around him, included lush, fleshed-out, three-dimensional renderings; everything looked so tangible, the player felt like they could reach into the screen and grab a banana.

The success of *Donkey Kong Country* was a significant hindrance to Sega's flagging sales; but while this game was in development, Nintendo's work on another console unwittingly spelled bad news for both companies.

Like Sega, Nintendo was eager to develop a disc-based, 32-bit console. But Nintendo didn't have the technological know-how to actually manufacture and encode discs. For this, it would have to look beyond its company—a huge taboo for Nintendo's corporate culture—and contract with a partner. It went into business with an expert manufacturer of discs and disc appliances: Sony.

Nintendo shared all of its game-design expertise with Sony, and in turn, Sony provided the hardware to develop a new console. It was, in essence, a Super NES, with games on CD-ROM, run on a powerful 32-bit processor. The two companies even collaborated as far as the prototype stage; they called their console the Nintendo Play Station.

Nintendo
Play Station

What happened next with that deal was very bad news, not just for Sony, not just for Sega, but ultimately for Nintendo, as well. The reclusive company, so used to going it alone, got cold feet after announcing the project in 1991. The very next day, Nintendo withdrew from the deal, leaving Sony in the lurch. Nintendo had decided to proceed with another cartridge-based console after all, and now Sony had sunk a fortune into research and development with no product to show for it and no way to recoup its investment. So Sony built it anyway.

Sony unveiled its revolutionary next-generation console, kicking off the race into 32-bit gaming: the Sony PlayStation. It was primarily an act of revenge against Nintendo, but it would hit stores around the

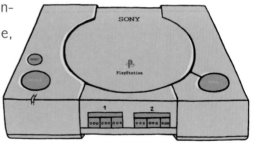

Sony PlayStation

same time as Sega's 32-bit Giga Drive project, which was now called the Sega Saturn. Worst of all for Sega, its $400 console was going to be undercut; the Sony PlayStation retailed for $300. It was a better, less expensive system, with more games available.

Sony also offered competitive rates for third-party developers to come aboard and make PlayStation games. Nintendo had jealously guarded its technology and the quality of its games by making third-party licenses prohibitively expensive and limiting how many games an outside developer would be allowed to make per year. But Sony welcomed developers with open arms (and low licensing costs), so a huge wave of future PlayStation games was already underway when the system launched in Japan in 1994. The first 100,000 PlayStations sold out immediately, and another 200,000 were rushed into production, selling out within months.

The Sony PlayStation was the last nail in the coffin for the Sega Genesis, and it effectively made the Sega Saturn dead on arrival. It also finally toppled Nintendo from the position of nearly unparalleled dominance it had enjoyed for 10 years.

HELLO
XBOX

A second head-to-head console war between new players leaves Nintendo out of the game... temporarily.

Minecraft; see page 116

"Nintendo 64!! Oh my god!!

"Thank you!"

"Oh my god!! Oh my god!!"

"Thank you!"

"Aaaahhhh!!"

"Yes!"

[both] "Yes!! Yes!! Yes!! Yes!! Yes!!"

The excitement was contagious. When a family home movie of a brother and sister unwrapping Nintendo's new

Nintendo 64

console on Christmas morning turned up on YouTube (around 10 years after that particular Christmas actually happened), the internet went as wild as the kids in the video. And it's easy to see why: the enthusiasm when the Nintendo 64 first came out was exactly that rowdy, and the fondness of our memories for that particular console is exactly that intense. But a closer examination of the history reveals the N64 was more of a letdown than we nostalgically care to recall.

With the success of *Donkey Kong Country* for SNES bolstering Nintendo's bottom line, the company elected to take another six months from its planned release date to fine-tune its next console...namely because it wouldn't launch it without a Mario game, and Shigeru Miyamoto was months behind schedule.

The N64's central processing unit, its 64-bit computer brain, came from Silicon Graphics—the same hardware the Stamper brothers had used to create the 3-D rendering of *Donkey Kong Country*. Miyamoto was learning to use this technology to create Mario in 3-D for the first time; for him, this entailed not only devising new ways for Mario to look and move, but figuring out entirely new game mechanics for how Mario explored. No longer limited to sideways scrolling in a flat 2-D perspective, the N64's processing power meant the world could spread out and Mario would be able to run in any direction, creating unexpected challenges. For one, where would the camera go? This wasn't just another game to dream up in the same league as all of his previous hits; this would require an entirely new dimension of play—literally—that didn't exist yet. Miyamoto took another few months still, even beyond Nintendo's initial six-month delay, but he delivered a game that changed everything, and the Nintendo 64 was finally able to hit Japanese stores in June of 1996.

"IT'S-A ME, MARIO!"

When players fired up *Super Mario 64*, they heard something no one had ever heard before: Mario's voice. The over-the-top Italian inflection—affected by an American voice actor named Charles Martinet, who has provided Mario's voice ever since—should have been embarrassing. But the minute they pressed start and heard "Let's-a go," fans embraced Mario's voice immediately.

Mario and Bowser

The new 3-D Mario came with a full set of moves. To explore his omnidirectional landscape, he did more than jump: he could double-jump and triple-jump, do backflips, and bounce off walls. He could even grab his long-time enemy Bowser by the tail, spin him around, and fling him away. Miyamoto applied the stylings of the *Legend of Zelda* series to *Mario*'s gameplay; the world was wide open to explore freely, but progress would be measured by completing tasks in a certain sequence, acquiring the necessary items and abilities before advancing. Mario could jump into any of a number of levels to explore, but some levels could only be unlocked or completed after others. Levels also had bonus items and stars for Mario to return and collect, games within games, making *Super Mario 64* endlessly replayable.

So what was the problem with the N64? For all of Nintendo's trailblazing 3-D rendering with *Super Mario 64*, *The Legend of Zelda: Ocarina of Time*, and several other games, the company was still programming them into cartridges. By this point each cartridge had the built-in memory card, but even so, games on disc were out there, with 10 times more memory, and Sony was already releasing them for the PlayStation. Nintendo liked cartridges because their data loaded faster, they were easier to manufacture in-house, and they were harder to rip off. But Square, a Japanese developer that had previously only made games for Nintendo, was developing *Final Fantasy VII*—the game that was destined to be its greatest—and it didn't want to limit its potential to a cartridge. When Square jumped ship and signed with Sony to release *Final Fantasy VII* exclusively for

PlayStation, the video game world took notice; others would follow. *Super Mario 64* and *Ocarina of Time* were huge, iconic hits, but in the long run Nintendo ended up releasing fewer than 400 games for the N64—fewer than any of its other consoles, and considerably fewer than the 1,000 or so that came out for PlayStation.

XBOX JOINS THE PARTY

Bill Gates, the cofounder of Microsoft Corporation, was fond of telling an anecdote about the industry: when the president of Apple, Michael Spin-

Bill Gates

dler, was once asked what other computer company he was most worried about as competition, his reply was Nintendo.

It was an unexpected answer. Today we're used to our all-in-one devices—laptops that can stream TV shows, video game consoles that browse YouTube, phones and tablets that can do everything a computer can do—but things weren't always like this. For a long time, the worlds of video gaming and home computing were mostly separate. Even though the average home computer had video games—from *King's Quest* on the original Apple Macintosh in 1984, to LucasArts' *Grim Fandango* on the Microsoft Windows PC in 1998—computers didn't pose much of a threat to video game consoles, or vice versa. Most families didn't even have computers during the '80s or much of the '90s, and the ones who did usually kept it in a home office or in a corner far from the TV, outside of the shared family room. And where the TV was kept, that's where the video game console lived; computers weren't about to take that space over.

But by the end of the decade, Sony had muscled its way to the top of the console business, outperforming Sega—whose fifth and final attempt at a console, the Sega Dreamcast, came and went without a splash, but actually innovated in ways that influenced future Sony and Nintendo systems—and Nintendo, which had faltered with its lackluster entry into games on disc, the Nintendo GameCube.

Nintendo
GameCube

Sony
PlayStation 2

When Sony unveiled the PlayStation 2 in 1999, anticipation from fans was so high, and Sony's confidence in the system was so great, that it got carried away with bragging about the system. With online connectivity, a built-in DVD player, and the adaptability to incorporate new software technologies as they came, Sony promised that the PlayStation 2 would knock the traditional computer from its comfy perch in family life.

Microsoft didn't like that one bit. Microsoft engineers and executives worried Sony could actually make good on its boasting...and what's more, the PS2 would be in the living room, hooked up to the TV, while the family's Microsoft PC gathered dust in another room. But if there are two things Microsoft had going for it, it was relentless competitiveness and a virtually bottomless bank account. The company immediately put a team together—comprised of James Allard, Kevin Bachus, Otto Berkes, Seamus Blackley, and Ted Hase—to fast-track the development and construc-

Microsoft
Xbox

tion of a console to fight back with. They called it the Microsoft Xbox.

The two consoles were released almost head-to-head: PlayStation 2 in 1999 and the Xbox in 2001. It was Super Nintendo vs. Sega Genesis all over again...but with two totally new players this time, while Nintendo ran a distant third, and Sega fell out of the running entirely.

Although the PlayStation 2 didn't launch with many games, leading people to suspect it would founder and fail, the games soon started coming. New installments of high-profile franchises from the original PlayStation like *Final Fantasy* and *Grand Theft Auto* made full use of the new system's capabilities and demonstrated that the PS2 had legs; it would go on to sell over 150 million units, becoming the world's best-selling video game console of all time. The Xbox, meanwhile, came right out of the gate with an exclusive launch game that would not only become a smash success, but would be tied to the Xbox's identity to this day: *Halo: Combat Evolved*. The world wasn't sure what to make of Microsoft as a video game maker, but with *Halo*, the Xbox earned instant respect.

Master Chief

Halo dropped the player into an immersive, first-person experience of gritty, science-fiction warfare. Master Chief, a silent, battle-armored foot soldier, quickly became the Xbox's own Mario—the character most associated with a console, the face of an entire brand. The game sold more than five million copies, and it inspired multiple sequels, novels, comic books, and web series.

MISSILE COMMAND

In a curious twist on the history of computers as a product of the military-industrial complex and early video games as missile defense simulators, the PlayStation 2 ran into a very, very unusual problem.

After Sony began selling the first million units in Japan, the government's Ministry of Trade announced it would limit exports outside the country; no individual could take more than two PlayStation 2s out of Japan, and any organization or wholesaler that wanted to order more than a certain amount would have to apply for a special export license.

NINTENDO ROARS BACK

Everything they did with the Xbox and PlayStation 2, Microsoft and Sony did again, bigger and better. Microsoft released the Xbox 360 in 2005, with graphics and a refresh rate so sharp that the system could only be played on a flat-screen, high-definition TV, and Sony launched the PlayStation 3 with a built-in Blu-ray player. They were in for a surprise, however. Never one to rush a product, Nintendo had been biding its time,

The reason why wasn't disclosed at first, but eventually the news came out: the graphics-rendering microchip in the PlayStation 2 was sophisticated enough, the Ministry of Trade believed, to be used for guidance systems in nuclear missiles. The fear was that a small government or rogue state, which might have rudimentary hardware like missiles and nuclear materials to arm them with, but not the sophisticated computer technology to control them, could buy up dozens or hundreds of PS2s, strip out the components, and launch an attack.

In the end, the export licenses were granted easily to anyone the Ministry of Trade considered a reliable customer, and the PlayStation 2 was sold throughout the United States and Europe.

developing new technology, designing new games, and planning its comeback. And the direction it was moving in was the biggest blind spot of the PS2 and the Xbox, with Nintendo making a break and pulling ahead again.

The Sega Genesis had elevated video games into the medium's adolescence, with an attitude of brashness that appealed to teens. The PlayStation 2 and Microsoft Xbox, in turn, brought big-name global brands in consumer electronics into a market previously dominated by small Japanese companies, boosting video games for the first time into a multibillion-dollar business, with games more advanced and complex than anything players could have dreamed of. That was their weakness.

The PlayStation 2 and Xbox controllers had multiple joysticks, directional pads, and a dizzying, confusing array of buttons. You practically had to be a trained expert to play.

MEANWHILE...MINECRAFT

Developed independently in 2009 by Swedish game designer Markus Perssun, *Minecraft*—the second-best-selling video game of all time—was purchased by Microsoft in 2014.

When Nintendo announced its new console coming in 2006, the Nintendo Wii, the launch game packaged with it was *Wii Sports*—a collection of simple games like baseball, tennis, bowling, golf, and boxing. At first glance, the graphics didn't even seem that good—hokey renderings of little plug-shaped figurines with bulbous, cartoon heads. But the key was the "Wiimote."

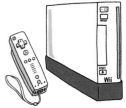

Nintendo Wii
& Wiimote

The Wii came packaged with a sensor to mount on your TV. Standing in the middle of your living room, holding the cordless Wii controller—the two-part Wii remote, or Wiimote as fans nicknamed it—you could point the wand portion at the menu screen, where a white-gloved hand would select your game, or move the cursor with the joystick under your thumb in the "nunchuck" component. Then all you had to do to play *Wii Sports* was move exactly as the sport you were playing. With the wand and nunchuck in your hands, you could put up your dukes to guard your face and throw punches, and just like that you were boxing. Swing the wand like a tennis racket, and your character executed a graceful overhand to match your own movement. Making the motions of rolling a bowling ball down the lane worked just as in real life—you could even put a spin on it, and if you pointed the wand poorly, your ball would end up in the gutter.

The simplicity of the Wiimote wasn't limited to *Wii Sports*; unplugging the nunchuck, the wand could be held sideways and operated just like an old-fashioned NES controller. Or, for a game of *Super Mario Galaxy*, pointing the wand at different parts of the screen controlled where Mario looked. Here was a video game you could play with your parents; with very little kids; with your grandparents; with someone who'd never even seen a Nintendo before. After years of ever larger and more complicated controllers, more overwhelming and confusing games, the Wii was a breath of fresh air and another triumph for Nintendo's philosophy of intuitiveness and inclusiveness...and of the pure spirit of play.

It paid off for Nintendo. After years of riding in the backseat behind Microsoft and Sony, Nintendo released a console that was less expensive than either one, with free online play (as opposed to the paid subscription services of the others), that was welcoming to every member of the family regardless of age or experience. The Wii sold so far above the Xbox 360 and PlayStation 3 that Microsoft and Sony didn't even consider it their competition; they insisted their only competition was each other. But the fact was that the Nintendo Wii sold more than the Xbox 360 and the PlayStation 3 combined.

Sony and Microsoft, savvy makers and sellers of technological hardware, soon came back with the PlayStation 4 and the Xbox One, respectively—both released in 2013, just in time for the holidays, and each

PlayStation 4

backed up by a wave of exciting new games. Nintendo had been left in the dust by these new consoles, but the company was already working on the next thing.

Xbox One

Rumors leading up to the announcement teased that Nintendo's next device would either be a new home console or a handheld system...but it turned out it was both. The Nintendo Switch was released on March 3, 2017, with a tablet device to hook up to your TV. The console could either be played at home or taken on the go; it was a revolutionary new way of interfacing with the video game experience, but it still had the recognizable Nintendo touchstones, like the small, simple controllers and the emphasis on fun and play.

Nintendo Switch

Everything about the Switch was new, but familiar. The controller, for example, looks and feels like the familiar Nintendo gamepad, but it can be taken apart and reconfigured several ways. Two joystick-and-button devices that come off the main controller can go on the sides of the tablet to play it like a handheld console, or they can be used as separate wireless controllers for two-player gameplay, with the tablet functioning like a tiny TV. That's a new way to do something familiar; it's an interface we've been using for decades, adapted into a totally new form.

There's no telling what the future holds for these three companies—Nintendo, Sony, and Microsoft—but they've already weathered and endured the trends that spelled the end of every other video game maker that preceded them. Could they eventually meet a similar fate as Atari or Sega, after all? Will another unexpected contender (like Sony and Microsoft were at one time) emerge to challenge them in the video game console business?

A better question might be whether home consoles will be how video games continue to be played in the future at all. Games on our mobile devices, games that we stream online with our computer or TV, and modular, multipurpose devices like the Nintendo Switch are already leading us to new ways of experiencing our video games. Compared to these, a box that sits on a shelf at home and only plays on your TV, with a controller that doesn't do anything else, seems positively antiquated.

Between these revolutions in interface across all our devices, and the growing processing power of computers, there's still no telling what video games will look like in another 10 years, let alone 20 or 30. The young video game players of today and the video game creators of tomorrow will be the ones answering those questions for us.

GAMING AND LEARNING

Educational video games are almost as old as the video game medium itself—it was always easy to see the educational potential in addictive play with elements of repetition, interactive cause and effect, and learning through trial and error—but the braininess of games blossomed at the dawn of the 21st century.

Brain Boost; see page 129

Educational video games have been around virtually
as long as commercial video games have been sold in
stores, with some of the earliest entries dating back
to the Atari 2600 and the first home computers in the
1970s. But with the boom of video games as a multibillion-dollar commercial industry, educational games
were about to blow up in a much bigger way.

Don Rawitsch was a college senior in 1971, teaching
an eighth-grade history class in Minneapolis as part of

Don Rawitsch

the school's student-teacher program. Looking for a fun way to teach kids about the harsh reality of the 19th-century American pioneers, Rawitsch came up with an idea for a computer game; he enlisted two other student-teachers, Paul Dillenberger and Bill Heinemann, as partners, and together they wrote a program called *The Oregon Trail.*

In a mostly text-based interface, the player guides a wagon party across the historic Oregon Trail to settle in the West, as countless pioneers did during the period of American expansion. The pioneers face setbacks, described in onscreen prompts, and the player types instructions to make choices on how to proceed—buying necessities like wheat and ammunition, hunting, distributing medicine, etc. As in the experience of the real-life pioneers, there are many ways for the player of *Oregon Trail* to die: there's hunger, thirst, exhaustion, and a litany of diseases including dysentery, typhoid, and cholera; you can drown; you can be shot; you can be stranded when all your oxen die; and you can even get bitten by a snake.

The Oregon Trail was such a hit with Rawitsch's students that, when the state started the Minnesota Educational Computing Consortium to develop educational software for the classroom, it hired the team to relaunch the game statewide. The new and improved version was shared freely across all the state's schools on the MECC's time-share network (a rudimentary form of the internet), and it was downloaded and played so many times that the MECC then produced a commercial version for sale in 1974. *The Oregon Trail* was the first great educational game and a favorite of schoolkids to this day in its many reeditions, updates, and sequels.

The Oregon Trail

LEAPING AHEAD

After spending six years trans-
forming Sega into the first
real competitor to Nintendo,
Tom Kalinske was ready for a
new challenge. At that time,
a company called LeapFrog had

LeapFrog

been making interactive educational devices for over a
year. Michael Wood founded the company after inventing the Phonics Desk, a prototype interactive device to
teach kids how to "activate" words and hear them read
out loud. It was exactly what Kalinske was looking for;
the executive had cofounded a company called Knowl-
edge Universe, and it merged
with LeapFrog in 1997. Leap-
Frog was primarily known for
interactive hardware like the
original LeapPad, a talking
book that read its own text out
loud when kids activated it with

LeapPad

a special pen device. Under Kalinske's direction, the
company became a maker of educational video games
as well. Today, in addition to its traditional phonic-and-
stylus readers, LeapFrog produces a full line of video

game consoles for kids in several age ranges, from 3 to 9—a home TV console called the LeapTV; a handheld console, the Leapster; a touch-screen video game tablet, the LeapFrog Epic; and an updated version of the LeapPad—all with the specific intent of helping kids read.

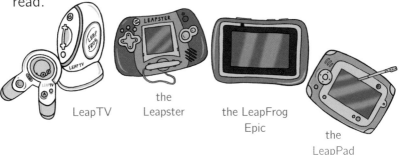

the
LeapTV   Leapster   the LeapFrog
Epic

the
LeapPad

BRAIN TRAINING

Games of mental stimulation aren't just for young children...as evidenced by the runaway success in Japan of Dr. Ryuta Kawashima's famous book, *Train Your Brain*. Dr. Kawashima, a neuroscientist and a professor at Tohoku University in the city of Sendai, believed that exercises such as games of memory, math, and puzzles could strengthen memory, rejuvenate the brain, and slow down mental decline in older people.

After leading Nintendo for decades, through its greatest period of growth and success, Hiroshi Yamauchi hand-selected his successor for the presidency of the company. He chose Satoru Iwata, a talented and beloved video game vision- ary who had joined Nintendo just two years before. Iwata was a devotee of Dr. Kawashima's *Train Your Brain* book and invited the neuroscientist to a meeting

Satoru Iwata

during the launch of the handheld Nintendo DS. The two men hit it off immediately, spinning ideas for hours and eventually coming up with the concepts for the *Brain Age* series of Nintendo DS games.

Dr. Kawashima, as seen in *Brain Age*

Dr. Kawashima came around on the value of video games, using his own research of brain scans and cog- nition tests to see how his players improved their performance. In the game, the floating, pixilated head of Dr. Kawashima himself challenges the player with logic, number puzzles, math problems, and memory tests, promising that 10 minutes of play per day will strengthen and rejuvenate the aging brain. The friendly, smiling digital avatar of Dr. Kawashima became a new familiar face for Nintendo, and the company successfully captured an entirely new audience of gamers over the age of 55.

Doctors and scientists are optimistic about the potential of the *Brain Age* series and similar games like *Brain Boost*, also for Nintendo DS, to combat the effects of Alzheimer's disease, a tragic condition that causes severe memory loss and impairment in the

Train your brain!

Brain Boost's scientist

elderly. However, by science's rigorous standards, proper research takes a long time, and the results have to be replicated in several separate studies before they can be considered conclusive. One concern that hasn't been dispelled is that these games don't adequately strengthen memory as a whole, but rather, they only train the brain at the specific game being played; in other words, the person who improves their score at a game like *Brain Age* may only be getting better at playing *Brain Age*, not actually improving their memory and cognition. While there's hope in this field, there simply hasn't been enough research into these games to know for sure if they really help. However, doctors and scientists also insist that all manner of mental exercise helps keep the brain healthy, just like physical exercise helps the body.

Duolingo's owl

A similar problem arises with *Duolingo*, the world's most popular app for learning languages. Functioning like a video game, the *Duolingo* app challenges its users to translate phrases in the language they're trying to learn, ranging from the very common ("How are you?" "I'm well, thank you; and you?") to the extremely unusual ("My hovercraft is full of eels."). Most of these unusual choices are taken directly from existing sources like novels, movies, and TV shows and are meant to keep users from getting complacent, with unexpected phrases providing an extra challenge and keeping learners on their toes.

Critics maintain that *Duolingo*, like *Brain Age*, primarily trains its users in how to win at *Duolingo*, not in actually learning about its subject matter. Whether this objection is accurate can only be tested by rigorous studies with replicable results.

Luis Von Ahn, a professor of computer science at Carnegie Mellon University who was born and raised in Guatemala, specifically wanted to help fellow Latin Americans learn English easily and cheaply. Carnegie Mellon is one of the United States' premier

Luis Von Ahn

technology institutions, and Von Ahn was a talented computer scientist who had already been awarded a MacArthur fellowship—an award so prestigious that it's nicknamed the "Genius Grant." Von Ahn used the funds from that award and other grants to finance his initial development of *Duolingo* as a Carnegie Mellon professor, working with a graduate student from Switzerland, Severin Hacker. *Duolingo* launched as a website in 2011, then as an app for iPhone

Severin Hacker

and iPad in 2012 and for Android in 2013. It became the number one app within the educational category on every platform, getting millions of downloads from users all around the world.

The success of *Duolingo* can be attributed to the appeal of gamification, the phenomenon where tasks such as learning or work duties are structured to progress through a series of levels and achievements, not unlike a video game. *Duolingo* starts out by teaching its user individual vocabulary words. Eventually the lessons level up to selecting the right words to fill in the blanks in a sentence provided, and from there to the challenge of translating an entire sentence, and even, for the most advanced users, practicing speaking the language out loud into the microphone on your device.

Educational games like *Brain Age* and *Duolingo* depend on the progression of video game structure. Gamification, on the other hand, consists of the opposite: applying the familiar principles of video games to transform real-life learning into a fun, satisfying, learning process. For many years—decades, even—parents and teachers despaired that these brightly colored, fast-moving, loud, addictive video games were shortening attention spans, reducing intelligence, cutting into homework time, and rotting young minds. But after two or three generations of kids were raised on video games and still managed to become accomplished, competent adults, society started to realize that video games weren't ruining the youth. In fact, if anything, video games may have done just the opposite—uncovered an effective new way of teaching.

The challenge for educators teaching through gamification is to incorporate these motivational factors of video games into their lessons, without importing the more negative side of video games, such as ultra competitiveness, aggression, and frustration. Done well, students learning through gamification can benefit from the trial-and-error mode of video games to be bolder in their thinking and unafraid of failing because dying in a video game is always followed by respawning.

LET'S CREATE NEW WORLDS
ON A PC

Home computers armed with modems, CD-ROM drives, and random access memory push video games in directions it takes consoles years or decades to match—yet they always come in second.

Utopia, see page 141

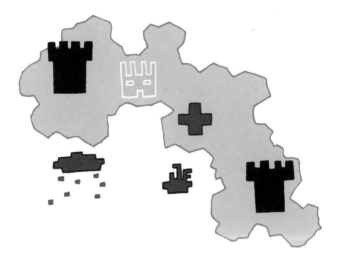

Until now, this book has focused on arcade video games and home consoles, siblings who were raised by the same parents—Atari and Nintendo. But parallel to their development, a cousin was growing up somewhere else in the neighborhood: computer games.

Way back when—around the time in 1976 when kids in arcades were busting bricks in *Breakout* and racing down the track in *Night Driver*, but wouldn't be shooting down *Space Invaders* for another couple of years—

Will Crowther sat down and wrote *Colossal Cave Adventure*, the world's first interactive text-based game.

In *Colossal Cave Adventure*, the player uses simple text commands and onscreen prompts to explore a cave for its treasure. There are no visuals whatsoever, just basic descriptions of the player's surroundings, to which the player responds by typing in commands for how to explore the space described. "Light torch," "Go north," and so forth. But for all its simplicity, *Colossal Cave Adventure* contained many, many firsts.

Not only was it the first text adventure game, it was the first adventure game of any kind, predating anything yet to be developed in the genre for arcades. In its focus on a descriptive narrative drawing on the player's imagination, it was also a precursor to role-playing video games, heavily inspired by the tabletop adventure game *Dungeons & Dragons*, which had been created only two years before. *Colossal Cave Adventure* also inspired the kind of text-based exploration adventure game referred to as a "multi-user dungeon," or MUD, an early online multiplayer experience, connecting players on distant computers via ARPAnet, the Advanced Research Projects Agency Network, which was the earliest version of the modern internet. In other words, the influence of *Colossal Cave Adventure* can be seen everywhere, from computer games to *The Legend of Zelda* to *World of WarCraft* and *Call of Duty 4: Modern Warfare* and other games played in a shared online world.

Many, many games followed in the footsteps of *Colossal Cave Adventure*'s text-based interface, but by far the most notable was a game that pioneered what no other computer game ever had before: graphics. Actual visuals. Onscreen art.

Roberta Heuer had grown up a shy girl with a vivid imagination. As a teenager, Roberta met Ken Williams, and she ended up marrying him and taking his name. Roberta Williams was a huge fan of text-based computer games when Ken came home one day with a brand-new Apple II computer. Checking out the new machine, Roberta realized its graphics capabilities could improve on the limitations of the games she was used to.

Roberta created and wrote—and, for the first time in

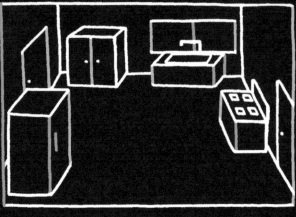

```
YOU ARE IN THE KITCHEN. THERE IS A STOVE,
REFRIGERATOR, AND SINK.
------------------------- ENTER COMMAND?
```

Mystery House

computer games, *illustrated*—a game called *Mystery House*. Ken went on to do the coding to bring the game to digital life. The Williams couple founded their own company to release the game in 1980, On-Line Systems, which they later renamed Sierra Entertainment.

As Sierra, the couple and their staff of developers went on to create dozens of popular games, including one of Roberta's most influential creations, the adventure series *King's Quest*. This led to a sci-fi spinoff, *Space Quest*; the cop procedural *Police Quest*; and even licensed games tying in to movies like *The Black Cauldron* and *The Dark Crystal*.

King's Quest, written and designed by Roberta and released in 1984, was a revolutionary entry in the graphical adventure genre for featuring more detailed graphics and more animation than any prior computer game, along with a compelling story about a lone knight saving the kingdom and rising to the throne. *King's Quest* and the other games of its ilk also pioneered a new "point-and-click" genre of computer game. There was still text input of commands, as players were used to—the knight, Sir Graham, could be instructed via text to walk or stop or pick up an object—but he could also be made to move with the arrow keys on the keyboard or by clicking on the screen with the mouse.

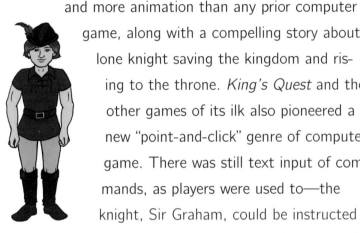

Sir Graham

By the end of the 1980s, Sierra, in one of its farthest-reaching and most forward-thinking innovations, began developing an online network. The Sierra Network, also called the Sierra Internet Gaming System, launched in 1991, with separate divisions dedicated to multiplayer online games, bulletin boards, and chat rooms. The Sierra Network was incredibly far ahead of its time, and in fact, it would go on to enjoy a notable reincarnation later in video game history.

Sierra, a massively successful video game developer and media company throughout the 1980s and '90s, ended up changing hands repeatedly, before eventually closing

Roberta & Ken Williams

down. But it wasn't a tragic ending; Roberta and Ken Williams earned their rightful place as living legends in the history of video games and computers, and they got to retire and enjoy all their success. As for Sierra itself, the company may have ended, but not before mutating into a surprising new form that lives on today.

Partnering with developer Valve, Sierra published the highly popular and hugely influential first-person shooting game *Half-Life*. It was one of the most popular games to play online on the Sierra Network, even as the network changed hands among several companies and had its named changed to the World Opponent Network, or WON. Eventually Valve itself bought WON in the early 2000s and used the one-time Sierra Network to begin testing its new project, an online game service that would change the world: Steam.

BUILDING WORLDS

By the 1990s, home computers—with their massive hard drives, processing muscle, and extensive memory—excelled at one genre of video game that consoles couldn't yet touch: the god game. That was the nickname given to simulation games dedicated to sprawling, literally world-building strategy.

It was a genre almost single-handedly inspired by the 1980 board game *Civilization*, created by a British designer named Francis Tresham. Inspired by the board game's pioneering "technology tree," requiring players to acquire items and develop skills in a specific order to build and oversee the growth of their empire, Don Daglow created *Utopia* in 1981. In Daglow's computer game, players each controlled an island and its population, keeping them fed, encouraging their industrial development, and competing against other players and the people of their respective nations.

Don Daglow

On the strength of his success Daglow intended to create a computer version of *Civilization* next, but he never completed it. Instead, a team of two developers, Sid Meier and Bruce Shelley, launched their version of the game for PC in 1991, starting a revolution, much like the restless people of the game's virtual nations.

The gameplay of *Civilization* spans thousands of years, from 4000 B.C.E. through the present day and into the distant future. Players must nurture the birth and growth of a human society, keeping it going in competition against rival civilizations (and rival players), encouraging its development, winning wars, and spreading its people across the globe.

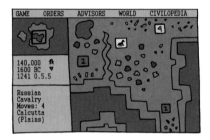

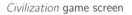

Civilization game screen

SimCity, smaller in scope than *Civilization*, actually came before, in 1989. Will Wright had been a young developer at the company Brøderbund, where he developed a game for the Commodore 64 console in 1984 called *Raid on Bungeling Bay*. The game, a warfare shooting game with an overhead view of the battlefield, included a feature for players to create their own maps. After *Raid on Bungeling Bay* was out in the world and he was used to

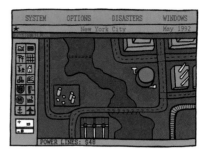

playing it, Wright found that the map-creating bonus was his favorite part of the game, so he deliberately developed a new urban-planning game

SimCity game screen

around that. *SimCity* was a game with no competition and no winning or losing, just the satisfaction of designing an interesting city.

For this reason, Wright's own employer, Brøderbund, and several other video game companies didn't believe *SimCity* would be successful and passed on it. When it was further developed and about to be published by a small start-up company called Maxis, Brøderbund finally saw its potential for fun and came back and partnered with Maxis to release *SimCity*.

Despite *SimCity*'s outsized reputation, it inspired a spin-off game even more beloved and influential—*The Sims*. *Sims* players zero in on the god game concept at a more microscopic scale and focus on a much more intimate setting—running a household of individual people, like a digital dollhouse.

CONSOLES LOG ON

Video game consoles couldn't keep up with the sprawling, world-building games of PCs, but as the technology became more sophisticated in the late 1990s, they caught up.

Since the first days of the Famicom in the early 1980s, Nintendo wanted its console to accommodate a modem, in case it ever became feasible to log on and play online. For each subsequent console, Nintendo always had the discussion again—put in a modem this time? But the answer was always no, not yet. That day would come by the end of the century, but for all its foresight, Nintendo wasn't the first to get there.

Sega Dreamcast did it. Following the failure of the Sega Saturn, the company tried to turn its fortunes around with the development of an incredibly inventive machine that would change everything. And in a way, it did; the Dreamcast was years ahead of its time, boasting several innovations that later became standard for other video game consoles...but not for Sega. The fate of the Dreamcast was tragic, and it would be the company's final attempt at manufacturing hardware.

The Dreamcast, released in 1998, came equipped with a modem for online gaming, and it was the home of *Phantasy Star Online*, the first home console version of a newly born genre of online multiplayer games. *Phantasy Star* opened the door for players at home to enter a vast shared online world, where all players' adventures took place together. *Phantasy Star* players on the Dreamcast could meet, collaborate with, and compete against other Sega gamers anywhere in the world.

MULTIPLAYER GETS MASSIVE

Though it was the first multiplayer game on a console, *Phantasy Star* was reined in by certain limitations—for one, players didn't have total freedom to explore the world of the game but had to follow a set course of gameplay. But the PlayStation 2, released just a year after the Dreamcast, changed that. PlayStation 2 players in Japan soon discovered the open world of *Final Fantasy XI*, a game they could wander through at liberty. This new mode of free-range game was called the MMORPG—the massively multiplayer online roleplaying game.

An even cleverer pioneer of an open world MMORPG was *EVE Online*, developed in Iceland. In this PC game set in outer space—a galaxy with 7,500 star systems, traversable through warp shortcuts—some 250,000 subscribers follow no guided narrative whatsoever. Players are free to pursue their own goals. The only stories that unfold in the game are those created by the gamers themselves: building corporations, buying and selling in-game products and services (which translate to real-world money), generating wealth, stealing wealth, and even carrying out assassinations and invasions.

Shortly after *EVE*, Blizzard Entertainment launched the fourth game in a series that had enjoyed only modest success in its first three installments. But in this latest entry, the game's designers—Tom Chilton, Jeff Kaplan, and Rob Pardo—spent an inconceivable five years on development and testing before finally launching the game in 2004 as an MMORPG for PC and Mac: *World of WarCraft*. After buying the game, players subscribe to the shared online world for $15 a month, joining the truly staggering population of over 12 million other people in the land of Azeroth. There, taking the form of a barbarian or an elf or an Amazon warrior or a gargantuan beast or any other number of creatures, players explore, interact with each other, and come across missions and quests of all sizes and complexity levels. This kind of alternate online universe would have been impossible for players to visit even when dial-up modems were the main way to access the internet; but by the early and mid-2000s, when games like *WarCraft* were launched, high-speed broadband internet had entered most homes and was becoming commonplace around the world.

World of Warcraft character

Online adventure gaming, whether massively multiplayer or just solo, was now fast becoming the standard. In the very near future, new developments in the MMORPG genre, downloadable games, in-game customization, and entirely new platforms and technologies would open up the world of video game creation to all-new masses of people. And it would all begin with a telephone.

NEW CENTURY,
NEW RULES

Between social networks, app stores, and crowd-funding platforms, all the dominoes were in place for the 21st century to witness an avalanche of user-generated content—for the first time, virtually anyone was free to create video games.

Super Meat Boy, see page 157

In the first decade and a half of the 21st century, the video games landscape became more and more competitive. A video game company like Nintendo had to worry about an electronics manufacturer like Sony and its PlayStation. The electronics manufacturer had to keep an eye on a computer maker like Microsoft and its Xbox. And now, the computer maker would have to watch its back against a cell phone. Apple unveiled the iPhone in 2007, and this powerful device would transform the industry once more.

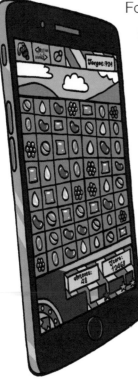

For years, cell phone makers like Nokia and Motorola had been laboring to make their devices lighter and smaller, while companies like BlackBerry moved in a separate direction with chunky, full-keyboard communication devices called personal digital assistants that offered office-related functions like email and a calendar. The iPhone combined all of that and more into one elegant, pocket-sized, touch-screen device. Apple effectively forced all its competitors to fall in line with the new style of smartphone or go out of business.

Interestingly enough, the product that Apple cofounder Steve Jobs most wanted to create was a tablet. But he knew that a touch-screen tablet was too new and unfamiliar, a device that the average consumer wasn't used to operating and wouldn't know how to use. He elected for his company to develop a more familiar object instead—a cell phone—incorporating Jobs's vision of touch-screen functionality in a way that would be more intuitive for new users to pick up on. A cell phone was a more indispensable object than a tablet; everyone already carried around phones. Even at a higher price than the standard cell phone, customers wouldn't feel they were splurging on a luxury "toy," like a tablet. And once they'd had a few years to learn the iPhone, to get used to its candy-colored onscreen buttons for apps and its revolutionary touch-screen take on portable computing, then Apple would roll out the iPad in 2010.

The App Store
on an iPad

The iPhone and iPad changed just about every-thing, but one of their more surprising reverberations was in the world of video games, through the creation of the App Store. Starting with the second model of iPhone, Jobs introduced the App Store, allowing developers outside Apple to create native apps—programs that live and operate directly within the Apple operating system on the iPhone and iPad.

For video games, this was a floodgate opening. Any aspiring video game developer, from a major corporation to a tiny one-person start-up studio, could create a mobile game, submit it to Apple, get it into the App Store, and see how they fared on the market.

BIRDS OF A FEATHER

Describing *Angry Birds* to someone who's never heard of it makes that game sound like an utterly ridiculous concept; and yet, not only have we all heard of it, we know very well how compelling and entertaining a concept it is. Developed by three young Finnish engineers—Kim Diker, Niklas Hed, and Jarno Väkeväinen—*Angry Birds* is a seemingly simple game of slinging the eponymous angry birds into crates full of pigs and causing as much destruction as possible. The Finnish creators had successfully developed mobile games for Nokia and other clients, earning enough capital to start their own company, Rovio Mobile, and develop an original idea. The product was *Angry Birds* in 2009, earning the Rovio team 50 million downloads in the first year alone.

Kim Diker

Niklas Hed

Of course, for every *Angry Birds*, there are countless stalled attempts that never get off the blocks. But eventually even Nintendo would join the fray, first with *Pokémon Go* in 2016, cocreated in partnership with the developer Niantic, a year later with its flagship hero in *Mario Run*, and once again with *Mario Kart Tour*.

Jarno Väkeväinen

Of course, Nintendo may have entered this new gaming arena because it could see the writing on the wall—that mobile games spelled the end of handheld consoles. Even the best handheld console is limited in what it can do versus a web-enabled device with a massive hard drive that can stream online games, play video, make phone calls, send emails, and take pictures.

BUILDING STEAM

Some of the history that we've covered has been about corporate intrigue and dollar-chasing commerce, but the overwhelming majority of these stories have been about individual people who loved video games and who saw games that engaged them and were motivated to try making their own.

But naturally, the bigger the video game business became, the higher the barriers of entry. Video games were epic productions costing millions or tens of millions or even hundreds of millions of dollars to create, with sophisticated animation and sound, running on reams of processing power, starring huge casts of famous actors, raking in sales in the billions of dollars—it wasn't as simple anymore for an aspiring young video game creator to see something cool and say, "I bet I could try that." The App Store democratized the process somewhat, lowering that barrier of entry; Steam would lower it further.

Steam was born on the Sierra Network, where Valve hosted *Half-Life* alongside games by Activision and other developers, until Valve bought the network. From there, Steam grew. And grew. And grew.

Valve launched Steam in 2003 on the World Opponent Network (formerly Sierra) as its new dedicated online service for hosting games. In 2004, *Half-Life 2* was released exclusively via

Half-Life 2 game screen

Steam. Before long, Valve was signing deals with publishers to host their online streaming games and downloadable purchases on Steam, with the service providing cloud storage and multiplayer gaming. Today, Steam accounts for 75 percent of online digital distribution of games.

The true magic of Steam, however, is in Steam keys and the Steamworks API. Steam keys allow third-party developers—anybody who isn't Steam itself or one of its official partners—to sell games on the network.

With the addition of a Steam social network, including voice and chat features, Steam has become a booming online community where players, spectators, and indie game developers hang out, play together, buy and sell their own games, and stream content. It's a welcoming enough platform that Steam has racked up over 150 million total users; as many as 18 million people all over the world are on Steam at any given moment.

However, making games costs money. The computer hardware and memory it takes to build a game are costly, and once you have everything you need, writing all the code still takes a lot of time—so much that it's a full-time job. Video game creators sit at their computers diligently, writing code and testing their game for hours at a time, every day, for several months. Financing this sort of undertaking, without the indie developer going broke, falling behind on rent, or practically starving, is too expensive for anyone but the very wealthy.

Enter Kickstarter. Founded in 2009, the online crowdfunding website lets anyone launch a campaign to raise money for a specific project. The creator of a Kickstarter campaign spells out the dollar amount they need, agrees to a time limit to raise that amount, and promises exclusive rewards in exchange for donations at various levels, including, for example, own⟋

new game when it's ready and other bonuses. If ⟋

amount (or more) is raised, the project is funded; if ∟

campaign falls short, everyone keeps their money and

the project is canceled.

Dozens of indie video game developers have successfully

financed games through Kickstarter and other crowd-

funding platforms and subsequently completed their

games and put them up for sale on Steam, Xbox Live,

and other platforms.

Additionally, Kickstarter has enabled the financing of

other video game-related media, including the documen-

tary *Indie Game: The Movie*, which follows the progress

of three very successful independent games—*Braid*, *Su-

per Meat Boy*, and *Fez*—each created by small teams,

and the online documentary series *Tropes vs. Women in

Video Games*, produced and hosted by Anita Sarkeesian.

Tropes vs. Women aired on YouTube and examined the

lopsided representation of female characters in decades'

worth of video games, which began all the way back in

Donkey Kong.

ART AND THE FUTURE OF

VIDEO GAMES

With nearly 50 years of the commercial video game industry in the history books, the debate remains on whether they generate a genuine emotional response or they simply shorten attention span and rot the brain.

Gran Turismo Sport; see page 163

When we look at video games as a booming, lucrative industry, with dozens or even hundreds of people involved in creating a single game—from the designers, writers, and artists down to teams of special effects engineers, coders, and testers—it's easy to lose sight of these games as self-expression and dismiss them as large-scale, corporate-driven mass entertainment.

It might take hundreds of people to make a movie, but the significance of its emotional message, when it rings out with clarity and resonance, is credited to the director, the screenwriter, and the actors. Nor is a movie necessarily any less personal or intimate a piece of work because it's supposed to turn a profit at the box office and earn back what it cost to make.

Video games, like any good art done in the mediums of film, television, publishing, or any other profit-driven industry, combine art and commerce; they're designed to please a mass audience enough to sell in large numbers. But that doesn't mean they don't reflect an intimate feeling held and valued by its creator.

Every video game creator profiled in this book started out as an individual with an idea, or a feeling, or a reaction to another game that influenced them. All of these video games were created in conversation with each other, and each one sprang from the interests, curiosities, passions, and frustrations of its creator.

In 2012, New York's world-famous Museum of Modern Art (MoMA) planted a definitive stake in this discussion by acquiring 14 crucial games throughout video game history, including *Pac-Man* and *EVE Online*, and launching a new curatorial department that would grow and exhibit this collection. In announcing the acquisition, MoMA stressed the value of video games as art and interactive design and set out a list of 40 seminal games the institution intends to collect, for starters, specifying *Spacewar!*, *Pong*, *Donkey Kong*, *Super Mario Bros.*, *The Legend of Zelda*, *Street Fighter II*, and more.

In Italy, the Video Game Museum of Rome houses a collection of games, from the Magnavox Odyssey through today's games, even hosting tournaments and publishing its own magazine about the industry, *VMag*. Berlin's Computerspielemuseum, which moved into its permanent home in 2011, displays period arcade machines like *Pong* and console games from the Odyssey, the Famicom, the PlayStation, and more. But surely the rarest collection of all belongs to Moscow's Museum of Soviet Arcade Machines, which houses only games made behind the Iron Curtain, so to speak, in the former Soviet Union. Some of these are in working order, but others, like the classic Russian game *Sea Battle*, were recovered from landfills or cobbled together from the parts of several nonworking machines, refurbished purely for display and not play. The museum's collection also includes classic Soviet games with irresistible titles like *The Giant Turnip, Tank-Training Area, Snaiper-2,* and *Buttle-Planes.*

As institutions go, museums look backward—but universities look ahead and educate a new generation of video game creators. Although it's a relatively new development at the start of the 21st century, more and more schools are building up their game departments, offering classes and even majors for aspiring video game developers. Students at New York University's prestigious Tisch School of the Arts can now major in game design at the newly formed Game Center, learning about everything from the design of video games to the business side, and even critical studies of games. At the University of Southern California, students can pursue a bachelor's degree in interactive entertainment, which focuses not only on consoles and arcades, but keeps up with the latest in emerging technologies. The University of Utah, where Nolan Bushnell went to school when he first discovered *Spacewar!*, offers undergraduate and graduate courses in video game design.

The evolution of video games throughout history has

proceeded so fast, there's no telling what they'll look like in another 10 years, let alone even further ahead. Virtual-reality technology, for instance, existed for decades without entering widespread use, limited mainly by its exorbitant cost. But all of a sudden, with companies like Oculus Rift innovating ways to manufacture cheap VR headsets and wearable technology like haptic gloves, virtual reality is blossoming all around us. Its potential for video games and everyday use is so enormous that we can only guess at all the ways it might enter our lives in the near future. Sony already sells a PlayStation VR headset for the driving game *Gran Turismo Sport* and others, and Google's own brand of VR headset can be used with Google Earth to "fly" around the globe. Researchers at the Program for Anxiety and Traumatic Stress Studies at New York's Cornell University are experimenting with a form of VR video game to ease post-traumatic stress disorder in veterans of combat in Iraq and Afghanistan.

In the brief time between this book being written and when it's published, many more developments will be underway, and not

PlayStation virtual reality headset

only in virtual reality. All technology thunders ahead continuously. Sometime in the near future—probably not in this decade, maybe not even the next (though who can say)—we're poised to witness a breakthrough in quantum computing. Instead of being limited to the binary 1 or 0 calculating power of bits, quantum computers—powered by quantum bits, or "qubits"—will rely on the "superposition" concept of quantum theory. In simpler terms: a bit can be a 1 or a 0 but can't be both at the same time; a qubit can. Seems imposible, but that's the nature of quantum physics, the science of energy in particles at the subatomic level. And when a bit is freed of the binary restriction, its computing power multiplies virtu-

diagram of a qubit

ally infinitely. Quantum computing will revolutionize technology even more dramatically than the invention of the microprocessor did, when computers that used to be the size of your classroom gave way to machines that were not only faster and more powerful, but small enough to fit on your desk and, later, in your pocket. There's absolutely no telling how quantum computing will impact video games—all we know is that it will.

For decades, technology has changed so fast that the only constant factor is change itself—the evolutionary leaps that have transformed technology so radically. Yet for all the advances in hardware, and software, and game design, the chain of communication being transmitted from one generation of video game creator to the next remains unbroken—and that unbroken chain isn't the technology, it is the creative exploration and self-expression that sparked the idea for each video game. It's a singular conversation that can be traced back nearly 70 years; the same conversation will no doubt extend for 70 years to come, and far beyond. However we play in the future, the creators of tomorrow are being shaped by the video games you play today. Maybe even by the games *you'll* create.

GLOSSARY

bit Short for "binary unit," meaning information encoded as either a numeral 1 or 0. Bits are the smallest individual pieces of information at the heart of all modern computing.

cartridge Interchangeable plastic case housing the ROM of a video game, allowing a home console like the Atari 2600 or the Nintendo Entertainment System to play a wide variety of different games.

code Computer language that instructs a machine in the execution of a video game or other software. A video game is designed first as a story, with its visual art, sound, and gameplay functions; then all of that information is translated into code and stored on a chip in a cartridge, on a disc, or online for streaming and download. The video game console reads code and translates it back into the form of a game for you to play.

CPU Central processing unit, the electronic circuitry that functions as a computer's "brain." The CPU performs all of the computer's information processing and control operations.

disc A silvery disc used to contain information such as a video game and other software and read by laser in the console device. CDs, DVDs, and Blu-ray Discs are discs commonly used for video games, music, and movies; LaserDiscs and MiniDiscs are larger and smaller versions, respectively, and are now discontinued.

microprocessor A microchip, or a small grouping of a few chips, containing a single integrated circuit that performs all the functions of a computer's CPU.

RAM Short for random access memory, a form of computer memory storage in an integrated circuit. As opposed to ROM, which is slowed by the physical limitations of its storage medium (for example, spinning a disc), the computer retrieves and interprets RAM at a consistent speed regardless of where the data is located within the computer's memory.

ROM Short for read-only memory, information that a computer can read and execute but typically cannot change. ROM is physically encoded in a circuit when the chip is first manufactured, or stored on interchangeable devices like floppy disks, cartridges, and CDs.

IF YOU WANT TO BE A
GAME DESIGNER

NORTH AMERICA

The Art Institute of Vancouver
Vancouver, British Columbia,
Canada

Carnegie Mellon University
Pittsburgh, Pennsylvania, USA

Game Center at the Tisch School of
the Arts, New York University
New York, New York, USA

Savannah College of Art and
Design
Savannah, Georgia, USA

Toronto Film School
Toronto, Ontario, Canada

University of Southern California
Los Angeles, California, USA

University of Utah
Salt Lake City, Utah, USA

Vancouver Institute of Media Arts
Vancouver, British Columbia,
Canada

EUROPE

Darmstadt University of Applied
Sciences
Darmstadt, Germany

Istituto Europeo di Design
Milan, Italy; Madrid, Spain

LISAA—L'Institut Supérieur des Arts
Appliqués (LISAA School of Art &
Design)
Paris, France

Oxford Royale Academy, University of
Oxford
Oxford, England

Seeway—Escuela Superior de Diseño,
Animación, Comunicación Digital y
Fotografía; Universidad San Jorge
Barcelona, Spain

Somerset College
Somerset, England

South-Eastern Finland University of
Applied Sciences
Kouvola, Finland

Technische Hochschule Köln (Cologne
University of Applied Sciences)
Cologne, Germany

Uppsala University
Uppsala, Sweden

ASIA

Communication University of China
  Beijing, China

Department of Game, Tokyo Polytechnic University
  Tokyo, Japan

DSK International Campus
  Pune, Maharashtra, India

Game Creator Department, Nihon Kogakuin College
  Tokyo, Japan

HAL College of Technology & Design
  Osaka, Japan

OCEANIA

Media Design School
  Auckland, New Zealand

Monash University
  Melbourne, Australia

University of Technology
  Sydney, Australia

AFRICA

Friends of Design, Academy of Digital Arts
  Cape Town, South Africa

Vega School at the Independent Institute of Education
  Johannesburg, South Africa

SOUTH AMERICA

SENA—Servicio Nacional de Aprendizaje (National Vocational Training Agency)
  Bogotá, Colombia

MORE BOOKS ABOUT
VIDEO GAMES

Bertoli, Ben. *101 Video Games to Play Before You Grow Up: The Unofficial Must-Play Video Game List for Kids.* Lake Forest, CA: Walter Foster Jr., 2017.

Hansen, Dustin. *Game On! Video Game History from Pong and Pac-Man to Mario, Minecraft, and More.* New York, NY: Feiwel and Friends, 2016.

Luen Yang, Gene. *Secret Coders* series. New York, NY: First Second, 2015. www.secret-coders.com.

Parkin, Simon. *An Illustrated History of 151 Video Games: A Detailed Guide to the Most Important Games.* London, England: Lorenz Books, 2014.

Ryan, Jeff. *Super Mario: How Nintendo Conquered America.* New York, NY: Portfolio/Penguin, 2011.

Saujani, Reshma. *Girls Who Code: Learn to Code and Change the World.* New York, NY: Penguin Random House, 2017. www.girlswhocode.com.

Ryan, Jeff. *Super Mario: How Nintendo Conquered America.* New York, NY: Portfolio/Penguin, 2011.

INDEX

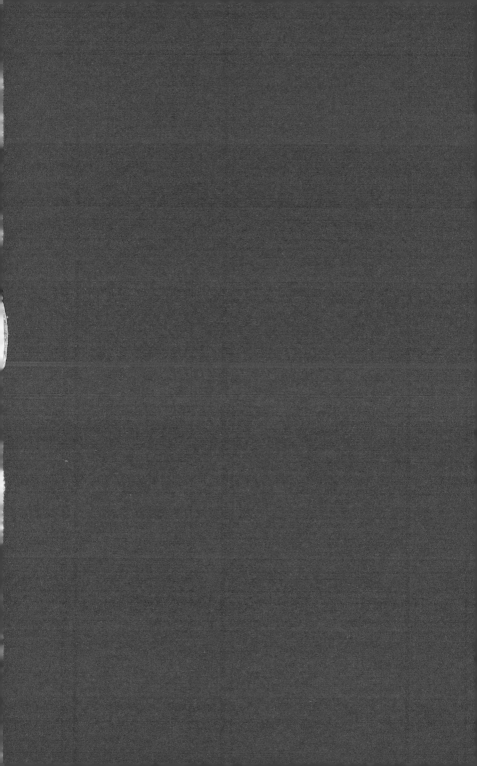